❧ *To* ❧

❧ *From* ❧

505 Quick Tips to Make Your Home

SenseSational®

Books by Terry Willits

101 Quick Tips to Make Your Home
Feel SenseSational

101 Quick Tips to Make Your Home
Look SenseSational

101 Quick Tips to Make Your Home
Smell SenseSational

101 Quick Tips to Make Your Home
Sound SenseSational

101 Quick Tips to Make Your Home
Taste SenseSational

Creating a SenseSational Home

For information about Terry Willits' speaking schedule
or SenseSational® Home products, please send a self-
addressed, stamped business envelope to:

SenseSational Homes, Inc.
P.O. Box 70353
Marietta, Georgia 30007
Telephone (770) 971-SENS
Fax (770) 971-0561

505 QUICK TIPS
TO MAKE YOUR HOME

SenseSational®

TERRY WILLITS

GALAHAD BOOKS
NEW YORK

Contents

101 QUICK TIPS
TO MAKE YOUR HOME
LOOK
SenseSational

— ⚜ —

He has made everything

beautiful in its time.

Ecclesiastes 3:11

Introduction

— ❖ —

$\mathcal{G}$od has given us eyes as windows to his world. Much of how we interpret life comes from what we see. And because we spend more time in our homes than perhaps anywhere else on earth, making them pleasing to our eyes can greatly affect our outlook on life.

Beauty is all around us. Every glimpse gives us a chance to notice something lovely. But since we are able to take in so much of the world at one time, it is easy to get distracted and fail to focus on the magnificent beauty right before us.

May the following tips inspire you to open your eyes to the beauty around you and bring a few fresh touches to your corner of the world — your home. Keep in mind, sometimes the smallest bits of beauty mean the most. God bless your home as you bring beauty to it!

Terry.

101 Quick Tips
To Make Your Home
❧ LOOK ☙
SenseSational

Wake up to the beauty around you.

*O*pen your eyes to the beautiful world God has created and discover what delights you. Notice the rainbow of colors and vast array of shapes and sizes and textures in nature. Let God's awesome creation inspire you to create a home that is pleasing to your eyes.

2

Begin a "my favorite things" box.

*U*se a decorative shoe box or hatbox to collect favorite items like trims, fabric swatches, ribbons, paper napkins, stationery, or other colorful memorabilia. This box will help you discover the most appealing color scheme for your home.

Color your world.

*G*od, the Master Artist, has painted beautiful colors on his outdoor canvas. Which colors please you the most? Color shapes every sight and influences every emotion. Surround your private world in the rainbow of your choice. You are the artist. Your home is your canvas.

4

Start a "dream" file.

*C*ollect pictures from your favorite home magazines for creative inspiration and future reference. File your clippings by room in an accordion file or a pretty notebook with clear vinyl sheet protectors. As patterns emerge in what catches your eye, you will begin to discover your decorating style.

Be on the lookout.

*O*bservation is one of the best ways to train your eyes and learn what pleases you most. Tour model homes in newly developed neighborhoods. Wander through furniture showrooms. Visit decorator showhouses. Go on home tours. Take your camera and a notebook, documenting anything you love.

6

Make home where your heart is.

*Y*our home should reflect the personalities, passions, and priorities of those who live there. On a piece of paper, list the personalities, passions, and priorities of each member of your family. Ask God to help you convey these as you decorate your home.

Make your front door friendly.

*Y*our front door is an outsider's first impression of your home. A pot of flowers, a wreath, a welcome sign, a fresh coat of paint or varnish, shiny hardware, clean light fixtures, a brass kick plate, or a pretty doormat all say welcome!

8

Shine on!

*F*or a long-lasting shine, wax freshly polished or new brass hardware (lacquered or unlacquered) with a quality lotion-type automobile wax. Let dry and buff with a soft cloth.

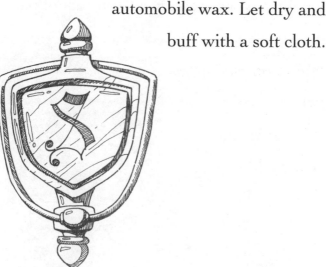

Glitter with glass.

A clean window allows you to fully enjoy the beauty beyond it. Clean your home's windows inside and out at least once a year, using warm water and vinegar as a cleaning solution. For sparkling appeal from the street, remove the screens on your front windows.

10

Get rid of grungy garages.

If your garage is the first place you see when you arrive home, try to keep it orderly. Stain a concrete garage floor a dark color to hide oil and dirt. (Stain won't peel or chip like paint.) Paint garage walls with a durable, semigloss paint so that you can wipe away any marks.

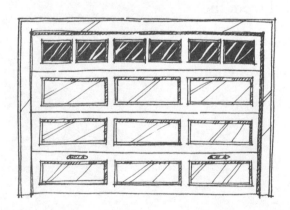

11

Clean it up by clearing it out!

*Y*ou cannot have beauty without order. Disorder distracts the eye. Clearing the clutter in your home will bring beauty to the forefront. Take advantage of organizational books and stores that feature organizational tools. Focus on one small area at a time. If organization is not your bag, ask an organized friend to help you get started.

12

Clean as you go.

*A*rrive at a practical compromise for cleanliness and sanity. If things are orderly and lovely to look at, a little dust or dirt won't be as distracting.

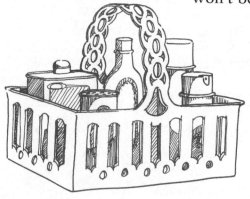

13

Begin with something beautiful.

*I*f you are wondering where to start to make a room pleasing to the eye, begin with what you have and love. Then work your way up, starting with the floor, furniture, walls, windows, and, finally, accessories.

14

Let it flow, let it flow, let it flow.

*F*ind one beautiful fabric or wallpaper for your main living area that has a pattern and colors that you love. Use this as the color palette for your entire home. Other rooms may only use one or two colors from this palette, but it will provide a smooth transition between rooms.

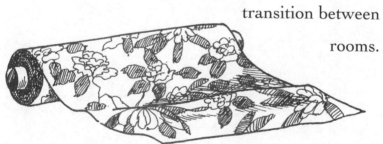

15

Try it before you buy it.

*B*efore buying yards of fabric or rolls of wallpaper, put the pattern on trial. Tape a large sample of your selection to a wall in the room in which you plan to use it. By looking at it and living with it for several days or weeks, you will be better able to determine if the pattern is right for you, possibly avoiding a costly mistake.

16

Welcome with color.

*P*lace a favorite piece of artwork, a hand-hooked rug, or a cozy wing chair in your entrance to introduce your color palette and to hint at the collage of colors yet to come.

Unite with white.

To allow a smooth transition between rooms, paint all trim on windows, doors, and moldings the same neutral color. Consider using a high- or semigloss, white oil-base paint. (White works well with all colors, and oil-base paint is the most durable for woodwork in your home.)

18

Paint it pretty.

Paint is the least expensive way to transform a room — but before you break out the roller, buy a quart of the color you have selected and sample it on a piece of poster board or foam-core, looking at it in the daytime and night-time. Use an eggshell or satin finish on walls and semigloss or high-gloss finish on trim. For an added touch, paint the inside of a closet to match the color of the walls.

Keep your head up!

*F*or heightened interest, stir one cup of the color paint you use on your walls into a gallon of white ceiling paint. When painted, the ceiling will slightly reflect the wall color. For an airy touch, paint a ceiling sky blue with clouds. For instant intimacy, paint the ceiling to match the walls.

20

Have fun with faux.

Experiment with different painting techniques to give a custom look. Sponge paint, marbleize, or stencil walls, furniture, or floors. A little paint and elbow grease can go a long way toward turning a room from mediocre to marvelous.

Let there be light!

*L*ight was the first element created by God; it is energizing, welcoming, and helps us to see the beauty around us. Use three-way bulbs in lamps to alter a room's atmosphere. Place a spotlight on the floor behind a plant or folding screen for indirect light and dramatic shadows. Hang picture lights to warm the colors of paintings. Use track or recessed lighting to high-light specific areas.

22

Seek the unique.

When selecting lamps, consider wiring an object into a lamp such as a brass or silver candlestick, a porcelain teapot, or a ceramic vase. A lamp shop can wire and mount almost any object onto a base. Select a pretty shade and decorative finial for a lovely custom lamp at a reasonable price.

Redress a lamp.

*U*pdate an old lamp with a new shade. Customize your shade by covering it in fabric or banding it with trim or fringe. (Many lamp stores offer this service.) Top off your lamp shade with a decorative finial.

24

Tie on a tassel.

$\mathcal{D}$ecorative tassels add a touch of color and class. Try hanging one from a lamp, a candlestick holder, a ceiling fan, a piece of artwork, or a key in a chest or secretary.

Create instant impact.

*D*ecorate your living room around a focal
point such as a fireplace, a cherished piece
of furniture, or a window with a garden view.
If possible, have your sofa face the focal
point or have two love seats flank it.

26

Keep it looking good.

*C*onsider applying stain-resistant finishes to light-colored upholstered furniture or to carpet or rugs in major traffic areas. Although these finishes will need to be reapplied after cleaning, they will help reduce soil and keep things pleasing to the eye.

Move it!

*R*earrange furniture for a new look,
making sure your favorite pieces are placed in
positions for you to enjoy. Move furniture into
groupings to create conversational areas or to
take advantage of views.

For coziness, draw
furniture in a few feet
from the walls. For
interest, place a sofa
on a diagonal.

28

Keep it cozy.

*I*n the winter, place a big basket of seasoned logs beside your fireplace. Summerize your fireplace with a decorative painted screen or a large basket of flowers or plants.

Entertain elegantly.

*U*se an old linen press or armoire to house television and stereo equipment. If the doors will remain open, remove them and rehang them in reverse so that the decorative sides will show.

30

Create a homey hearth.

$\mathcal{W}$arm up your mantle with a favorite collection, a beautiful piece of artwork, a decorative mirror, or a welcoming wreath.

Warm your home with wood.

*D*etermine which woods please you the most and provide the look you want. For an eclectic feel, tastefully mix a few finishes. For a rich look and luster, refinish a dull piece of old furniture and add new hardware.

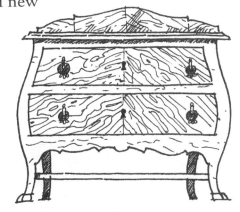

Create a clever coffee table.

$\mathcal{F}$or a unique, one-of-a-kind coffee table, find an old dining table with character and cut down the legs. Or find an interesting base and top it with a piece of heavy glass. Sturdy trunks work well too, as well as provide extra storage space to help keep clutter to a minimum.

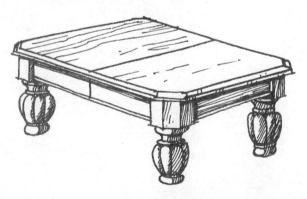

Store memories by the bowlful.

*P*ut a big bowl or basket on your coffee table and fill it with family photos that haven't yet been filed into albums. Not only is it a fun and easy accessory, it's a great conversation starter or memory jogger.

34

Freshen up with flowers.

*B*ring God's bountiful beauty into your home with a colorful bouquet of flowers. Make it a ritual when you go to the grocery store or farmer's market to pick up a bunch. Select those that appeal to you and go with your color scheme. They will lift your spirits as they please your eyes.

Cluster a collection.

Make it a fun hobby to collect a particular type of object that appeals to you — candlesticks, porcelain, pottery, bunnies, brass, vases, teapots. For visual impact, display the collection together.

36

Beautify your bookshelves.

*A*dorn your bookshelves with beautiful books. Place all hardback books together, removing jackets and pulling spines flush to the edge of the shelf. Stack large books horizontally on shelves or a coffee table. Place a pretty book on a plate stand, letting its cover face forward.

Accent it.

*F*or a splash of color, paint a contrasting or accent color behind your bookshelves. Before you do, though, test the color on a piece of foamcore and slip it behind the bookshelf to make sure you like it.

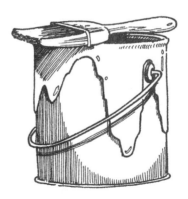

38

Create one-of-a-kind bookshelves.

*F*or a clean, dramatic look, fill your bookshelves with something other than books: all baskets, all colored glass, all wooden artifacts, all hats.

Browse through beautiful books.

*C*ollect beautiful books with photographs of places you have visited or things that you love, marking your favorite pictures with fabric ribbon. Display the books on a coffee table as a lovely reminder of your past or your passions. When you have a brief moment, sit and browse through your books and get lost in their beauty.

40

Charm with chairs.

*I*ntrigue the eye with the unpredictable. Unify two different style dining room or kitchen chairs by upholstering them in the same fabric. Or, let wing chairs stand in place of the usual end chairs. Vary matching chairs by recovering or slipcovering seats with different fabrics.

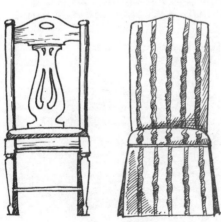

Break it up!

A tasteful mixture of furniture makes any room more interesting and pleasing to the eye. Breaking up a matching set of furniture lets each piece's beauty stand on its own. Try using a bedroom dresser for a buffet service in the dining room or using a bedside chest for an end table.

42

Go on a treasure hunt.

*S*earch flea markets, junk shops, antique shops, and estate sales for beautiful bargains. It doesn't cost anything to look! If something catches your eye the minute you see it, there's a good chance it reflects your decorating style.

Make the ordinary extraordinary.

*M*ix dinnerware. Collect pretty dishes and glasses that work well together. Combine your grandmother's china with goblets from a flea market. Mixing fine things with less expensive ones gives both priceless charm.

44

Create casual elegance.

When decorating your dining table, be creative and mix finishes. Combine flower-filled terra cotta pots or wicker baskets with crystal or silver accessories such as candlesticks. The eclectic combination will intrigue the eye.

Bring God's beauty indoors.

$\mathcal{P}$lants are an inexpensive way to give life, color, and warmth to any room. A hearty plant like a philodendron, pothos, or peace plant only needs to be watered once a week and fertilized with plant food once a month. Use spray-on leaf polish to keep plant leaves shiny and healthy.

46

Let your chandelier take center stage.

Enhance your chandelier by topping its bulbs with miniature shades, which are available in many colors, sizes, and styles. For a custom look, cover the shades with fabric, paper, or paint, and finish them off with trim. Soften the look of a chandelier's chain link by covering it with a shirred sleeve of fabric.

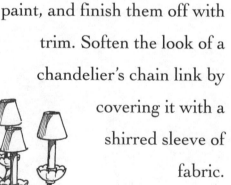

Switch it.

Replace ordinary electrical switch plates in visible places with more decorative ones. Buy quality brass switch plates, paint wood switch plates to match trim, or cover switch plates with wallpaper used in the room.

48

Cluster candleholders.

*U*nify a group of candleholders by using only one color for all candles. Although you can put together all sizes and shapes, stick to one or two materials: wood, brass, crystal, or silverplate. If a candle is too narrow for the holder, wrap the candle's base with a small fabric doily or a rubberband to add bulk and make it fit. Use elegant eighteen-inch candles for special occasions.

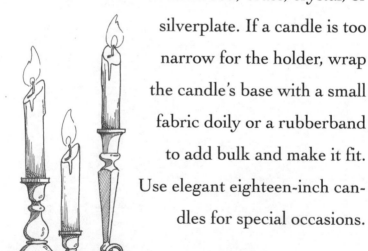

Dim it!

*D*im the lights and light a candle when you sit down to dinner, even when dining alone. This gracious gesture takes just seconds, but sets the tone for your meal and your mind-set.

50

Add a special sparkle.

For a flickering focal point in any room, place a large pillar candle on an Oriental wood base and surround it with a hurricane globe.

51

Make magic with mirrors.

A mirror can visually expand a room and lighten and brighten a space with its reflection. Have a beveled glass mirror cut for an old, large frame. Or, for instant impact, collect a variety of smaller, interesting mirrors from flea markets and assemble them into a collage on a wall.

52

Update kitchen cabinets.

New hinges and knobs can bring life to old kitchen cabinets. Try ceramic knobs that color coordinate with your kitchen accessories. Display tableware by replacing a few cabinet doors with glass doors. Or simply leave doors off cabinets, paint the interior cabinet walls, and have open shelving.

Make appliances appealing.

*I*deally, appliances should visually coordinate with the kitchen decor. If they don't, epoxy paint can be used to change their color. Change the front of a dishwasher by slipping

an inexpensive piece of laminate in its place. For an extra touch, have a pretty design handpainted on the laminate.

54

Beautify your burners.

*I*f you have an electric stove top, enhance your burners with enameled cooktop covers. Available in several colors, they save clean-up chores and create extra workspace while hiding unattractive burners.

Clear it off!

*I*nstead of hanging everything on your refrigerator doors, place an attractive bulletin board in an unobtrusive but convenient spot to hold information or homemade artwork. If you do use your refrigerator for display, edit it often, and make it as pleasant as possible. Use acrylic magnetic frames for refrigerator photos.

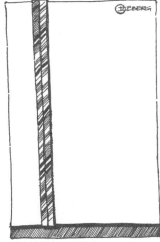

56

Keep countertops clutter-free.

$\mathcal{D}$isplay only utensils and portable appliances that are functional and beautiful; store all others. If it's time for a new appliance, consider an under-the-counter model to give your kitchen a cleaner look and increase work space.

Fascinate with food displays.

*F*ind creative and beautiful ways to display food items in the kitchen. Store flour, sugar, coffee, and tea in lovely canisters. Buy a pretty cookie jar to store cookies. Put dried, colorful pastas in oversize glass con-

tainers. Pour spices into small apothecary jars and arrange on a wood rack. Fill colored or clear glass bottles with flavored oils and vinegars.

58

Show it off.

*H*ang a simple shelf across a kitchen doorway or window. Load it up with attractive kitchen accessories that you love, but use less frequently. This will keep fragile items in view, but not in the way. Pot racks are a great way to display beautiful, but necessary cookware or baskets.

Display pretty plates.

*F*or a touch of charm, place decorative plates anywhere and everywhere. Prop them on plate stands. Hang them with either a wire hanger that slips onto the back of the plate or on a decorative rack that holds several plates at a time.

60

Buy a beautiful bed.

Save your pennies and buy a bed that suits your style — you'll enjoy it for years. Place your bed in a spot where you have the greatest view while lying in it. For a cozy look, try angling the bed from a corner. For a romantic look, raise any bed frame by placing it on sturdy blocks.

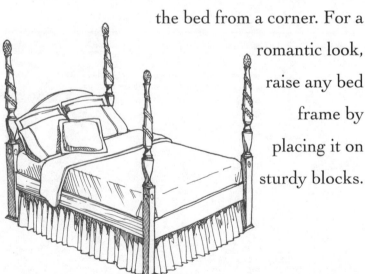

61

Mix and match fabrics.

*T*ake the guesswork out of decorating with ready-made collections of coordinated fabrics, wall coverings, and bed linens. To mix your own, look for remnant fabrics. Try mixing plaids, checks, stripes, polka dots, geometrics, or textured solids with a large pattern.

62

Double up.

*M*aximize your decorating possibilities using a duvet cover with a different fabric on each side. Flip it when soiled or simply for a new look. Give your dust ruffle a deluxe, designer touch by using one long and one short one. Or, if they are the same size, pull up on the top one and pin it to the box spring to create the same look.

Add pizzazz with pillows.

Use pillows to personalize any piece of furniture from a handsome chair to a hand-me-down sofa. When piling pillows on a bed, use a variety of different shapes, sizes, colors, and fabrics for visual interest. For a custom look, tie a ready-made pillow with a decorative tassel or fabric bow.

64

Keep your sheets sweet.

Use pretty, decorative sheets to beautify your home. They're well-priced, extra wide, and often have coordinating, ready-made pillows and comforters to adorn your bedroom. Or, for a pleasing table decor, turn a pretty sheet into a tablecloth and matching napkins.

65

Make it up.

*T*ry to establish a habit of making the bed as you leave it in the morning, and teach your family to do the same. Certainly, there are carefree times that call for an unmade bed; but more often than not, the simple task of bed-making sets the tone for the day and helps a bedroom look its best.

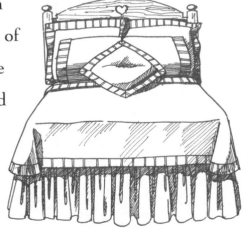

66

Put on a skirt.

A skirted table is an economical way to add color and coziness to any room while providing out-of-sight, but close-at-hand storage. Embellish a table skirt with cording, fringe, banding, or a ruffle. Top it off with a lace or fabric over-lay and a round piece of glass.

Express your heart with artwork.

*A*llow your passions to be expressed with your artwork. Sentimental treasures like christening gowns, heirloom lace, children's artwork, menus from special restaurants, or baseball caps can be framed for life-long memories.

68

Warm up a wall.

*H*ang colorful quilts, tapestries, or hook rugs on large walls, using a piece of wood and Velcro strips. Each can bring a touch of hand-made charm to any wall in your home.

Hang up your heritage.

$\mathcal{M}$ake your heritage a focus in your home by filling a hallway or stairway wall with framed photographs of family. Collect and frame black-and-white photographs of ancestors to keep track of the family tree, marking relatives' names in permanent, black ink on the back of each frame.

70

Keep it at eye level.

When selecting artwork, balance the visual weight, color, and scale of the artwork with that of nearby furnishings. When installing artwork, hang at eye level. (In a hallway, eye level would be when standing; in most other rooms, eye level would be when seated.)

Angle your art.

*F*or a friendly, casual look, prop a piece of artwork atop a mantle or chest rather than hanging it. Or mount a high chair rail with a groove to rest artwork on. When leaning several pieces together, vary height and sizes. Angling art keeps decorating flexible and fresh looking.

Frame your favorite faces.

*R*emember, relationships are the most important part of life. Collect pretty frames and fill them with the faces of those you love. Groups of photos look best with frames made, at least partially, from the same material to visually unite them.

Decorate down under.

When accessorizing a sofa table, don't forget to decorate beneath it too. Use large plants, stacks of big books, baskets, old leather luggage, or anything unique that will lend warmth and charm.

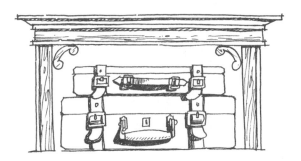

74

Have fun with a fan!

*J*azz up a ceiling fan by painting the blades to match walls or a colored ceiling. Or paint each blade a different color, handpaint them, or cover them with wallpaper. When feeling conservative, flip fan blades over to original finish.

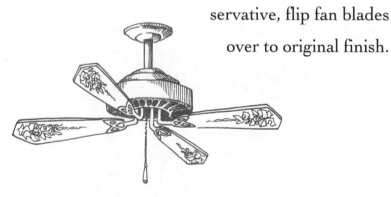

Put it on a pedestal.

*D*raw the eye to a special artifact or trophy by placing it on a pedestal. Raise objects such as a small lamp, clock, or picture frame to new heights on pedestals of stacked

books or wooden boxes.

76

Decorate with baskets.

*B*askets of all sizes, shapes, and colors can be used to decorate and organize the home. Adorn the tops of kitchen cabinets or the refrigerator with baskets. Fill them with magazines and place them in bathrooms. Use lidded baskets beside your kitchen phone and bed.

Make the most of your trash.

Natural, wicker trash cans are attractive and reasonably priced. Surprise the eyes by placing a pretty paper doily at the bottom of each. Try using a large, lidded wicker hamper for a kitchen trash can. It holds lots and looks warm and friendly.

78

Button up!

$\mathcal{U}$se covered or decorative buttons to enhance your pillows, window treatments, upholstered furniture, picture frames, or lamp shades. They're inexpensive, yet add an unexpected, unique touch that delights the eye when discovered.

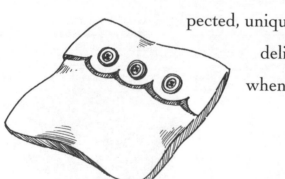

79

Create an "instant" antique.

*T*ransform a plain plaster or concrete sculpture into a beautiful accent piece by brushing or sponging on a wood stain finish or brown shoe polish. This trick will also turn homely, hardback books into rare and beautiful treasures.

80

Be unpredictable.

*A*dd a touch of whimsy or humor when decorating a room. Display a painting by a relative, a pair of cowboy boots, an old bicycle wheel — anything that makes you stop and smile.

Delight your desk.

*F*ind attractive, creative ways to display your necessary desk accessories. Consider using a small decorative vase to store pens or a silver toast rack to hold bills, letters, invitations, and correspondence.

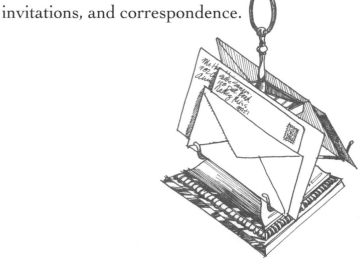

82

Think about it.

*K*eep a daily thought flip calendar by your kitchen or bathroom sink to inspire you at a glance and fill your mind with good things.

83

Top your table tastefully.

When accessorizing the top of any table, think of it as an empty canvas on which you can apply colors, shapes, and textures. Put low objects towards the front and tall ones toward the back.

84

Hide and seek.

To keep rooms fresh and pleasing to the eye, rearrange accessories frequently. By putting some away temporarily, and bringing others out, you will appreciate their beauty more.

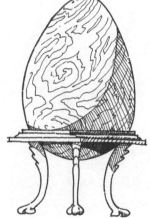

Discover hidden treasures.

*P*ull out those treasured wedding gifts tucked away in cabinets. Use a lovely silver dish for potpourri or a crystal bowl for a pretty candle. Don't overlook the family attic — you may uncover a hidden heirloom that can add a piece of family history to your home.

86

Contrast it.

*L*ike an outline to artwork, contrasting colors can please the eye and add punch to a room. Try colorful pillows on a neutral sofa or dark lamp shades in a room with light walls. Use contrast cording or banding on upholstery, window treatments, or pillows.

Make your windows wonderful.

*W*indow treatments should provide privacy and enhance a room without blocking outside light, air, and beauty. Keep your window treatments consistent with your decorating style.

88

Simplify, simplify.

*D*on't overdo when decorating. The eye can only enjoy so much at one time. Edit what you see. What you leave out is as important as what you leave in. A simple bowl filled with one kind of fruit cannot be surpassed for beauty.

Pair it.

*B*eautiful objects arranged in simple symmetry draw the eye to them. When possible, buy two of the same accessory. This gives you the flexibility to show them side by side or use them in two different areas.

90

Brighten chores with friendly faces.

*H*ang an attractive bulletin board filled with photographs of family and friends above your washing machine. Their faces will brighten your day as you do laundry, and will remind you to pray for them.

Paint a piece
to beauty.

*R*evive an old piece of furniture by painting it. Bring life and charm to a room by painting an outdated kitchen table and chairs. Hand-paint a "ho-hum" chest with a happy design on its drawer fronts. Spruce up an old wicker rocker with a coat of pretty paint.

92

Light up the night.

Turn on your front porch lights at night for a friendly glow. Set prominent lamps on timers to welcome family home and keep thieves away. Use pretty night-lights in all your bathrooms to light the way for children, guests, and even yourself!

Keep it out of sight.

*S*tore all personal beauty products and appliances in bathroom cabinets. If space is limited, add a touch of charm and storage to the room with a small chest or cabinet.

94

Behold bottles of beauty.

A pretty wicker shelf in your bathroom
is the perfect place to display decorative
glass bottles of mouthwash, lotions, and
bubble bath.

Use natural objects to decorate.

A seashell by the bathroom sink can hold soap or jewelry while you wash. A knotted branch can be used as a rod to drape a casual window treatment. Bamboo shoots hung horizontally can hold bouquets of dried flowers and make wonderful wall arrangements.

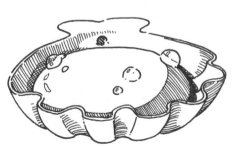

96

Spruce up the shower.

Enhance your bathroom with a pretty shower curtain. Buy a decorative one, or make one from a flat sheet, tablecloth, or fabric. Try adding color to a simple, white shower curtain by tying it to a curtain rod with grosgrain or other fabric ribbon bows that coordinate with bathroom decor.

Make a splash with color.

*B*ring color into your bathroom with pretty towels and throw rugs that coordinate with the room's decor. Don't stash color in a closet: hang towels on wall pegs or roll them up in a large basket beside the tub.

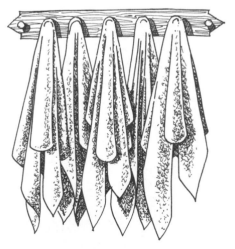

98

Cover it up.

To hide damaged or wallpapered walls or ceilings or to simply add visual interest and texture, put sand or stucco mixture in paint. Try upholstering a wall with fabric shirred on curtain rods or by stapling batting to the wall, then

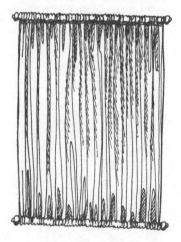

stretching and stapling fabric over the batting and finishing off the stapled edges with cording or trim.

Paint your paneling.

*P*ainted paneling lends clean, crisp, cottage charm to any room and makes a beautiful backdrop for colorful accessories. It gives a textural interest that smooth walls can't achieve. Paint existing paneling or add paneling before painting a room.

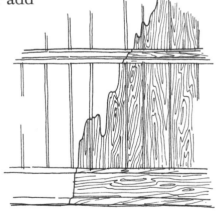

100

Take care of yourself.

*E*ach morning when you get up, get dressed, brush your hair, and apply some makeup. When you look good, you feel better. When you feel better, it affects your home's atmosphere.

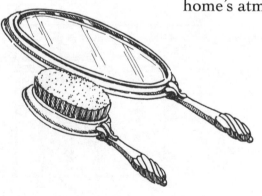

Create lasting beauty.

*I*nner beauty far outlives any of the fabrics or furnishings that fill our homes. Make it a priority to spend time in God's Word. As you communicate with him, he will inspire you with the most creative ways to bring beauty into your home. Remember, he is the One who makes everything beautiful in its time.

101 QUICK TIPS
TO MAKE YOUR HOME
❧ SMELL ☙
SenseSational

— ⚜ —

And the house was filled with the

fragrance of the perfume.

John 12:3

Introduction

— ⚜ —

*O*ne of God's sweetest gifts to us is the sense of smell. Similarly, one of the most satisfying things we can share with those who enter our homes is pleasant fragrance. Fragrance is a gift that will gratify today and linger in memories long after the scent is gone.

Whether we notice it or not, fragrance fills our lives. Every breath brings the opportunity to smell something wonderful. Unfortunately, it seems the only scents we stop to smell are those that are especially strong. The well-known saying, "Take time to smell the roses," suggests we should slow our lives down more often to enjoy the goodness of life.

May the following tips inspire you to smell the "roses" already in your life, as well as add some new blossoms to your fragrance bouquet. Keep in mind that the purpose of scents is to enhance your home, not overpower it. A few simple touches in each room are all you need. Have fun fragrancing!

terry.

101 Quick Tips
To Make Your Home
❦ SMELL ❧
SenseSational

Light up your life.

*L*ight a scented candle when you spend time with God. The fragrant smell will calm your spirits, bringing you pleasure and peace while you focus on him.

2

Welcome with a wreath.

*W*elcome loved ones to your home with a dried floral wreath or bouquet on your front door. A few drops of essential oil on the dried leaves will refresh its floral scent. For a special occasion, tuck fresh, fragrant flowers in a wreath of greenery.

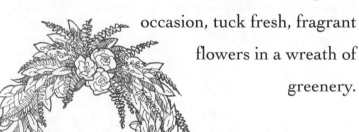

Pour it on!

*F*ill a watering can with sweet-smelling fresh flowers. Place it by your front door for a friendly, fragrant greeting.

4

Banish bugs.

To add scent to your home's exterior and to keep bugs away in warm weather, place highly-scented citronella candles by your entrances. They will welcome guests and ward off uninvited insects.

5

Greet guests with geraniums.

*I*n the spring and summer, a basket or pot filled to the brim with geraniums lends warmth and a pleasant fragrance to a sunny entrance. In the winter, bring them indoors to scent a cheery spot.

6

Smell the roses.

*R*oses are among the most preferred and perfumed flowers. Planting one in your backyard will ensure a bounty of beauty and scent for years. When doing other landscaping around your home, select some shrubs that are aromatic as well as attractive.

Live it up!

To ensure the most fragrance, cut fresh flowers from your garden in the morning, while it is still dewy. Extend the life and fragrance of fresh-cut flowers by adding a little chlorine bleach and sugar to luke-warm water. Trim the flower stems and change the water daily.

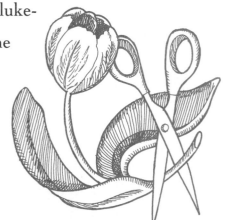

8

Bring joy with jasmine.

$\mathcal{S}$atisfy a sunny spot of your home with the sweet smell of jasmine. Hang a basket beneath a skylight, sit a pot on a windowsill, or embrace your mailbox with its vines and fragrant blossoms.

Wrap your windows with wonderful fragrance.

*B*uy a beautiful window box and fill it with cascading fragrant flowers and greenery. Consult your local garden center for suitable flowers and plants.

10

Clear the air!

*O*n a pretty day, open your windows and give your home a good, old-fashioned airing out. Let the fresh breeze sweep through your rooms. Take area rugs outside and shake them well to remove dirt, dust, and musty smells.

11

Filter it.

*C*hange your air filter frequently to clean your home of unhealthy, allergy-aggravating particles that your eyes can't see, but your nose can smell. Attach a Filter Mate to your air filter to scent your home.

12

Think green.

*F*ill your home with live plants. House-
plants can enrich your home life, not only by
pleasing your eye, but by cleaning the air
of impurities — they're God's free air
filter system!

13

Turn on the fragrance!

*F*or a safe and easy scent, place a lamp ring on a lamp's light bulb. Add a few drops of essential oil, then turn on the lamp to enjoy the fragrance for hours. To be welcomed with a pleasant-smelling greeting, set the lamp on a timer.

14

Treasure pearls of potpourri.

These tiny, perfumed pellets can be used in many ways. Place potpourri pearls in lamp rings, potpourri mixtures, dried flowers, simmering water, or a simple bowl to fragrance any room of your home.

15

Welcome warmly.

*L*et the sparkle and smell of a scented candle give a warm welcome that says "home." Place one in your front entrance and powder room to greet guests. Light one by your back door before loved ones arrive home, to let them know you are expecting them.

16

Share a sweet aroma.

*K*eep a small bottle of perfume in a basket
near the entrance where you greet family.
A quick spray will make you feel fresh and
will welcome those you love with a sweet
aroma well worth coming
home to.

Enjoy your pets.

 $\mathcal{B}$ athe dogs and change cat litter frequently. Your pets and all others who enter your home will appreciate your effort to keep things smelling pleasant.

18

Keep closets fresh as a forest.

Use cedar wood hangers to hang outerwear in your coat closet. They will repel moths and mildew while pleasantly scenting your garments. For an extra, unexpected whiff of fragrance, hide a cedar block or pleasing sachet on the top shelf of the closet.

19

Fire up!

*T*he smell of a wood-burning fire gives the instant impression of warmth and security. Prepare a fire in advance so you can enjoy its woodsy fragrance at the strike of a match.

20

Perfume with pinecones.

*P*ile a basket full of evergreen, cinnamon, or spice-scented pinecones by your fireplace. Toss one occasionally into the roaring flames for a burst of satisfying scent. To fragrance pine cones, simply dot them with a few drops of essential oil.

Scent with
heavenly herbs.

*H*ighly fragrant herbs can enhance a fire. To scent the room, tie tiny bundles of rosemary or lavender with twine, pile them in a basket, and every now and then toss a bundle alongside flaming logs.

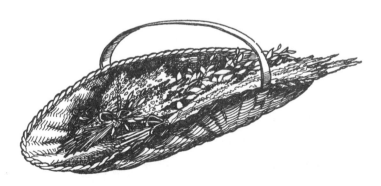

22

Provide pleasure with potpourri.

The natural beauty and fragrance of potpourri can enhance any room. Select an appealing, fragrant mixture and display it in a pretty bowl or dish. Revitalize potpourri with an essential oil. Store unused potpourri in an airtight glass jar in your pantry.

Fan the flames.

*P*lace a wooden bowl of pretty, pleasant-smelling potpourri by the fire so that the heat of the flames will warm the mixture and release its scent throughout the room. A handful of potpourri thrown in the fire will also delight your sense of smell.

24

Celebrate the season with scent.

Enhance potpourri with a seasonal touch. For a Christmas scent, add a few sprigs of holly, bright bunches of red berries, and cinnamon pinecones. For a fresh, spring fragrance, liven potpourri with lemon peels and dried yellow roses.

Begin a "love bowl."

$\mathcal{B}$it by bit, blossom by blossom, build a "love bowl" of potpourri. Pluck petals, leaves, and buds from bouquet stems as you discard them. Dry them and toss them in a bowl with a few drops of fragrant oil.

26

Save it with silica gel.

*D*ry flowers and preserve their vibrant colors by microwaving them with silica gel. Simply spoon silica gel to cover flowers and microwave them a minute at a time, testing the flowers' texture until crisp. Use your dried flowers for potpourri, adding a few drops of essential oil for fragrance.

Liven up with lovely scents.

*O*verflow a large vase in your living room with the vibrant aromas of lilac or lily of the valley. These flowers are especially fragrant and will delight all who gather together in your home.

28

Savor the wonderful scent of white.

*W*hite flowers are often the most fragrant. Fill a crystal vase with a dozen white carnations or roses and savor their scent and sophisticated simplicity.

Lemon up!

*D*ust wood furniture with a quality, pleasant-smelling furniture polish. For a fresh, lively scent, try lemon. Enhance the fragrance by stashing lemon-scented sachets behind a bookshelf or sofa pillow, or one to a doorknob or arm of a wooden chair.

30

Make a sachet in seconds.

*T*ake a pretty handkerchief or square of decorative fabric or muslin, spoon in a fragrant potpourri mixture, and tie it with whatever seems appropriate — a tassel, ribbon, raffia, or twine.

Rub it in.

*R*ub essential oil into the inside of a wood drawer, onto the back of a wood picture frame, or under a wood table. The unfinished wood will slowly absorb and release the oil's pleasant scent. Do not use essential oils on finished wood.

32

Make paperwork a pleasure.

*P*erfume your desk drawers with sachets or enhance your desktop with a single blossoming flower. Light a scented candle to inspire you while you work.

Send a scent.

*A*dd fragrance to your stationary by spraying cologne inside the lid or placing a sachet envelope in your stationary box. For a special scented gift, slip a sachet envelope or fragrant envelope of bath crystals into a card and mail it to a friend.

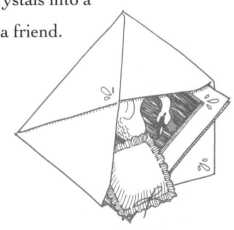

34

Share a cup and saucer
of scent.

*D*rop a scented votive candle in a pretty

demitasse or teacup. Place it on a saucer in a

spot looking for a touch of fragrant charm.

Make it a clean sweep.

To eliminate lingering smoky fumes, have a professional chimney sweep perform a safety inspection and clean your fireplace at least once a year.

36

Attract swarms of noses.

*L*ight a long-lasting beeswax candle. Its honeycomb texture and sweet honey scent make it most pleasing.

Bake a batch.

$\mathcal{M}$ake a big batch of cookie dough, roll it, and freeze it in wax paper. You can also use ready-made "slice and bake" cookie dough. Whenever the urge hits, bake a batch to fill your kitchen and your stomach with delight.

38

Go for the garlic!

*F*or a quick, delicious scent, sauté minced garlic and olive oil in a pan and let it simmer slowly. Whether you toast it on bread or toss it in food to stir fry, the great garlic scent is sure to satisfy.

Cook a turkey, chicken, ham, or roast.

The succulent smell of meat roasting is guaranteed to make your home smell cozy and your mouth water!

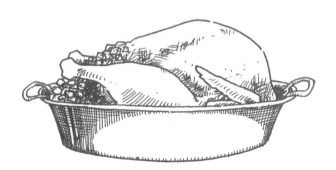

40

Pull out the crock-pot.

There's nothing like coming home to the smell of supper cooking — especially when you're the cook! Use your crock-pot to prepare simple, delicious-smelling dinners.

Wake up and smell the coffee!

*L*et the aroma of coffee brewing lure you out of bed in the morning. Make coffee the night before and set a timer to turn it on before your alarm sounds. For a special treat any time, grind fresh coffee beans with a dash of cinnamon.

42

Simmer some soup.

Make a big pot of your favorite soup and let it simmer on the stove. Savor the smell as it steams your kitchen and welcomes family home.

Sprinkle a scent.

Sprinkle carpet fragrance directly on carpet or add to vacuum cleaner bag. Then vacuum for an instantly clean-smelling home!

44

Pop up a steamy snack.

$\mathcal{M}$icrowave popcorn for a quick snack that will steam the air with its mouth-watering, buttery corn smell.

Bake bread.

*F*or bread baking without the bread making, buy frozen yeast rolls or loaves. Let them
rise and bake, and instantly your kitchen will
smell delicious. Or splurge on a bread oven —
it will save your time and knuckles and release
the scent of homemade bread.

46

Treat with sweets.

Make a cake or batch of brownies before dinner. Place them in the oven when you sit down to eat. The delicious smell of dessert cooking will tempt your nose just when your sweet tooth's ready.

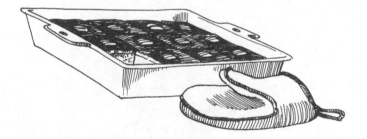

Light a luscious cake candle.

*A*vailable in scents like vanilla, cinnamon spice, and chocolate, yummy-smelling cake candles can be found in many gift and country shops. They last for days and make it smell as if you've baked for hours.

48

Scent a centerpiece.

*F*or a doubly fragrant treat, place a small jar of fragrant flowers in the center of a freshly baked bundt cake. It makes a creative centerpiece and will please all who partake.

Simmer a scent.

$\mathcal{S}$immer apple cider with cinnamon sticks, cloves, and orange peel for a spicy, fragrant beverage. If you don't have cider on hand, use boiling water. Although you can't drink it, the smell is just as enjoyable. You can also use a small potpourri burner to simmer a liquid fragrance.

50

Freshen up!

*R*emove lingering food aromas with an unscented kitchen candle or room spray. Both will neutralize odors in the air.

Refresh your refrigerator.

*W*ipe out your refrigerator and freezer with a mild fragrant soap and warm water before going on a big grocery shopping spree. Discard spoiled items. Restocking your clean, sweet-smelling refrigerator will be a joy! A box of baking soda will keep foods from absorbing other odors.

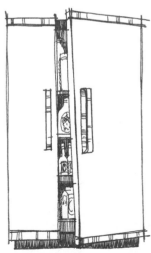

52

Fragrance with fruit.

Fill a bowl with the zingy zest of citrus fruit or soothing scent of apples. When a piece of citrus fruit looks "tired," cut it in half and grind it in your garbage disposal to replace unpleasant food odors with a lively, fresh scent.

Perfume your pantry.

$\mathcal{S}$tore a fruit-scented sachet envelope like apple, peach, or strawberry on a shelf in your kitchen pantry.

54

Breathe easy.

To make the smell of your trash cans, hampers, and diaper pails more tolerable, lay a sachet envelope beneath the plastic lining. You can also use scented plastic liners, scented disks that hang or stick, a sprinkle of baking powder, or an occasional squirt of scented spray.

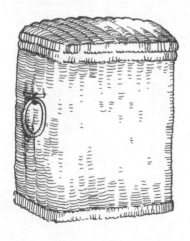

Buy a bouquet.

$\mathcal{S}$elect a bunch of sweet-smelling flowers for their scent, as well as their beauty. Scatter the flowers to spread their fragrance throughout your home. Place some in a pretty pitcher or teapot by the kitchen sink. Breathe in their friendly fragrance as you cook and clean up.

56

Cluster casually.

*F*ill a simple mason jar with a casual cluster of sweet-smelling daffodils. Tie a raffia bow around the jar's opening for a finishing touch. Share the joy of fragrance by taking a jar to a friend.

Place a pot in a sunny spot.

 $\mathcal{S}$ et a pot of fragrant flowers like paperwhites by a sunny window. They will impart a lovely fragrance and last longer than freshly cut flowers.

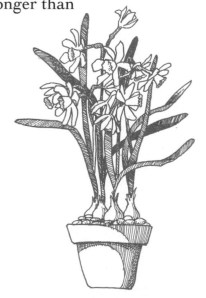

58

Enjoy the essence of herbs.

*E*nhance your kitchen with the healthy aroma of fragrant, fresh herbs like rosemary, basil, or lemon thyme. Decorate your kitchen with the delightful scent of an herb wreath, topiary, or bouquet displayed in a pitcher or hung from a pantry door.

Float your fragrance.

Create a scented centerpiece by filling a clear glass bowl with scented floating candles. Toss in a few rose petals to float. Surround the bowl with fresh flowers and greens. Enjoy the fragrant glimmer of the glowing candles.

60

Give guests their own glitter.

*U*se pretty, stemmed glassware or votive candle holders to hold small scented candles. Light one in front of each place setting. For a casual touch, use miniature terra cotta pots to hold scented votive candles. Spray paint the pots for color.

Perfume each place setting.

*P*erfume each place setting with a single scent-filled blossom or a petite bouquet of a few fragrant flowers. For a refreshing scent of interesting greenery, add fresh sprigs of mint. Collect and mix and match small, interesting vases or bottles. Just as each guest is unique, let each vase be.

62

Be twice blessed.

*L*ight a scented candle near fresh, sweet-smelling flowers. The fragrant flame will complement the flowers' scent and fill the air with perfume.

Remember with
a rose.

*F*or a scented delight at a special dinner,
lay a long stem rose in front of each place
setting. Tie a fabric ribbon with a handwritten
name card to each stem. Give guests their
roses as a fragrant memory of the meal.

64

Make a tussie-mussie.

*T*hread a cluster of fragrant flowers and fresh greens through the center of a small paper doily. Twist the underside of the doily around the stems and wrap with floral tape. Use them to enhance place settings or garnish desserts.

Fold in fragrance.

When setting your table, spray the underside of cloth napkins with a light mist of fragrance. For a scented napkin ring, tie a small fabric sachet with ribbon to each cloth napkin. Both touches give a fragrant surprise to friends and family when unfolding their napkins.

66

Create a sweet-smelling seat.

*T*ie a delightfully scented sachet to each
dining chair with a decorative tassel
or ribbon.

Grow a gardenia.

$\mathcal{L}$et the sweet smell of gardenia blossoms enhance your home. Or scent a sunny spot in your home with a dwarf lemon or orange citrus tree. Their broad evergreen leaves produce fragrant white flowers along with small citrus-scented fruits.

68

Fragrance fabrics.

*U*se a fragranced spray starch when ironing or lightly spritz a favorite cologne right onto your ironing board. The heat of the iron will permeate your fabric with fragrance.

Sleep tight.

$\mathcal{S}$lip a fragrant sachet envelope of vanilla, chamomile, lavender, or rose inside your bed pillow or decorative sham. Drink in the delightful aroma as you drift off to sleep.

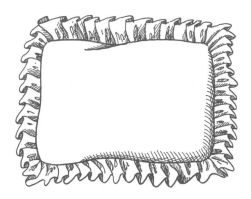

70

Fragrance linens lightly.

*C*hange your bedsheets as often as possible and launder them, as well as your clothes, with a pleasing, perfumed detergent. For a fresh fragrance in between launderings, lift your bedsheets and air them out. Spray them lightly with perfume.

Sprinkle your sheets.

On a warm summer night, before turning in, turn down your sheets and sprinkle them with a fragrant body talc. The perfumed powder will absorb moisture, delighting your nose while keeping your body dry.

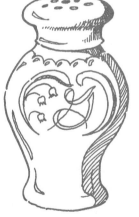

72

Store linens
with lavender.

When storing table linens, bed linens, and
towels, tuck a soothing sachet or a few sprigs of
lavender in between them. Lavender is a lovely
natural way to fragrance your linens while
repelling moths and other pests.

Perfume a pillow.

Spray a pretty throw pillow lightly with pleasant perfume or pin a decorative fabric sachet to it. Toss it in a spot where the scent can be enjoyed.

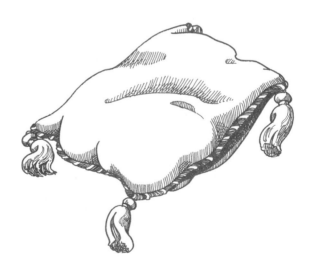

74

Suspend a scent.

*H*ang a bouquet of colorful fresh or dried
flowers from a poster bed or ceiling beam.
Hang decorative sachets from doorknobs
or furniture hardware.

Enjoy a bedside blossom.

A simple rosebud will enhance the air you breathe while you drift off to sleep and as you wake up. For an easy bedside arrangement, cluster colorful blossoms of delicate, sweetly-scented freesia in a small vase or pitcher.

76

Show off a single stem.

*I*n a bud vase, display a single stem of a pink-and-white stargazer lily. Select a stem that still has several closed buds on it. They will

gradually open over several days and slowly release their delicate scent.

Save your spot with scent.

*U*se a small sachet envelope as a scented bookmark in your Bible or the latest literature beside your bed. The fragrance will make reading so enjoyable you won't want to put the book down!

78

Fragrance a flicker.

To add scent to an unscented pillar or votive candle, dot a few drops of essential oil beneath the wick before burning. Light it, and enjoy the scent as long as the oil lasts.

Collect pleasing perfumes.

*C*ollect a few of your favorite perfumes and display them on a pretty tray on your dresser or vanity. Each day, spray one on that most suits your attitude and attire. For the ultimate luxury, use a lovely, tasseled perfume atomizer to mist on your fragrance.

80

Stick with pins and needles.

Use a scented pincushion made of a firm, fabric sachet to display pins and needles. Every time you puncture the pincushion or pull out a pin, the cushion will release its lovely fragrance.

81

Slip in a sachet.

Slip a sweet-smelling sachet envelope into your clothing drawers. Every time you reach for a garment, your spirits will be lifted. Surprise those you love by hiding scented sachet envelopes in their dresser drawers: men usually prefer spicy scents; young children like fruit scents.

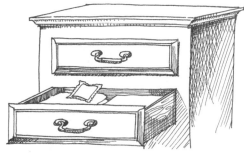

Line drawers in luxury.

*F*or a splurge of scent, line your dresser
or desk drawers with pretty, perfumed papers.
Rubber cement the paper in place. To replenish
the fragrance, spray a few squirts of
perfume on paper.

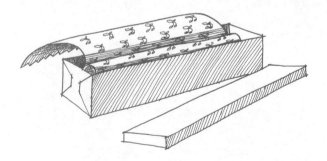

Be my guest.

What's more welcoming than a wonderful fragrance? Greet guests to your home with bedside flowers and a small gift basket filled with perfumed products to scent their bodies.

84

Have sweet-smelling feet.

*U*se cedar shoe trees or clear plastic boxes with sachets to store your shoes. Both will keep your feet smelling sweet and your shoes in tip-top shape. To absorb bad odors and moisture, occasionally sprinkle shoes with a fragrant powder mixed with baking soda.

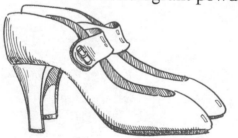

85

Hang it up!

$\mathcal{U}$se scented padded hangers to bring pleasant fragrance and shoulder protection to your nicer garments.

86

Stash a scent.

*L*ike a squirrel stashes nuts to savor for a later time, stow away surprises like scented soaps, lavender bundles, or cedar blocks in your off-season clothing to fragrance and protect it.

Pack a perfume.

$\mathcal{S}$tore sachets in unused luggage. Next time you travel, keep the sachet in your suitcase to keep it smelling fresh.

88

Spray away!

*P*lace a can of scented room spray in a visible spot in each bathroom of your home. Celebrate the seasons by changing the scents of your sprays. Gardenia in the spring. Pine in the winter.

Strike a match.

The charcoal smell of a burnt match can instantly override unpleasant odors and neutralize a room's fragrance. If you choose to spray air freshener after lighting a match, a light spray is all you will need.

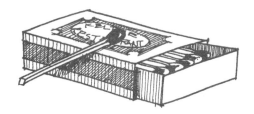

90

Soak in a scent.

When drawing a hot bath, fragrance your bath water with a lovely scent. Give yourself time to soak, savor the smell, and thank God for the many blessings in your life. For a lively, zesty smell, float several rings of thinly sliced lemon in your bathwater.

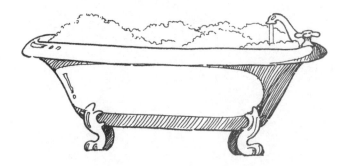

Soothe with scented candles.

*D*im the lights while bathing, and burn a scented candle beside your bathtub. The fragrant flicker will quiet you. Place the candle in a safe spot and let young children enjoy its soothing scent during their bath time too.

92

Mist in menthol.

*F*or a menthol treat, tie a bouquet or wreath of eucalyptus to your showerhead with a few strands of raffia. Moisture from a steamy, hot shower will release its stimulating scent.

Scent your seashells.

*A*dorn your bathroom shelves with scented seashells. To fragrance, soak small shells in essential oil or dot larger shells with a few drops of oil in their centers.

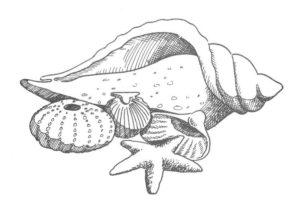

94

Plug it in.

Purchase an appealing room freshener that plugs into a standard electrical outlet. After you plug it in, forget about it! It is safe and easy and will fragrance any room for weeks.

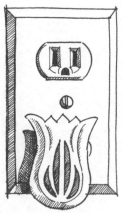

Scent a tank.

*F*ragrance and clean your toilet bowl with one of the many products available. Whether they hang on the side of the bowl or drop in the bottom of the tank, all give a whiff of freshness.

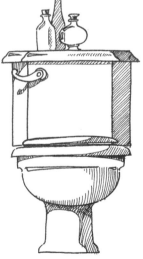

Dish up delightful soaps.

Fill a pretty dish in your powder room with small scented soaps. Family and friends will enjoy the fragrant treat as they wash their hands. Let children pick their favorite fragrances and shapes for their bath soaps. They will lather up with delight.

Select similar scents.

When choosing products to clean your home or body, notice the fragrances that please you most. The more products of the same scent you use, the more enticing that fragrance will be.

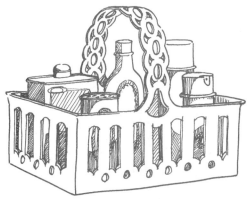

98

Avoid morning breath.

*D*o yourself and those you love a favor by fragrancing your breath with a refreshing mouthwash every morning.

Give it away!

When wrapping gifts, top them off with a touch of fragrance. Tie a rose, sachet, or cinnamon stick in the bow.

100

Lather in loveliness.

*B*efore crawling into bed at night, clean your body by lathering up with scented soap and rinsing in a quick hot shower or a long warm bath. Top yourself off with a sprinkle of favorite-smelling bath powder.

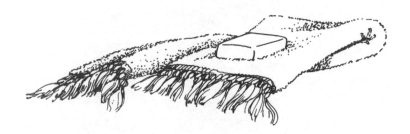

101

Fill your home with his fragrance.

The most satisfying and long-lasting scent in any home is the spiritual fragrance released from a Christ-filled heart. Fill your heart and mind with God's Word and allow the "sweet aroma" of his life to fill your home.

101 Quick Tips
To Make Your Home
❧ FEEL ☙
SenseSational

The wise woman builds her house, but with her own hands the foolish one tears hers down.

Proverbs 14:1

Introduction

— ⚜ —

$\mathcal{T}$ouch is the sense at the deepest root of our emotions. It is unlike any other sense in that it can be stimulated by every inch of the body — God has covered our bodies with approximately five million receptors to experience touch.

This powerful, yet delicate sense affects nearly everything we do in our homes. We touch people. We touch things. Every touch can bring a blessing to where we live, whether it be a gentle kiss, a warm hug, a tender stroke, a comfortable chair, a hot bath, or a cozy quilt. Unfortunately, the busier our lives become, the less time we take to enjoy touch.

May the following tips inspire you to slow down enough to enjoy the comforting touches that already fill your home, and motivate you to discover new touches as well. A simple touch can mean so much. Treasure God's gift of touch in your home.

Terry

101 Quick Tips
To Make Your Home
❧ FEEL ❧
SenseSational

1

Get in touch
with touch.

*A*waken your sense of touch in the home you create. Notice the feel of fabrics and furnishings as you touch them. Use the hands God has given you not just for laboring, but for loving. Make every effort to fill your home with loving touches of comfort.

2

Make the first step satisfying.

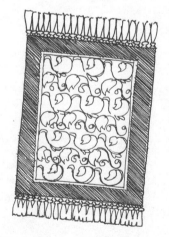

*G*reet guests with a pretty area rug inside your front door. It will be their first touch of comfort as they step into your home. Select a rug with a background color or busy pattern that will camouflage dirt. For comfort, and to prevent slipping, place a vinyl mesh grip beneath it. For extra cushion, use a piece of carpet padding in place of the mesh grip.

3

Give homecoming hugs and kisses.

A cheerful homecoming shows love, respect, and admiration. Try to be home to welcome family at the end of their day. Stop whatever you're doing and greet them at the door with a warm hug or kiss.

4

Welcome visitors warmly.

*G*reet visitors to your home with a warm hug or firm handshake. For an extra touch of sincerity, give a double-handed handshake. Such thoughtful gestures of touch instantly convey love and acceptance and put others at ease in your home.

Please sign on the line.

$\mathcal{D}$isplay a beautiful guest book and a pen on a table by your front door. Invite visitors to sign it as they leave your home. This little book will soon hold cherished memories of special times spent with friends and family in your home.

6

Beautify with blankets.

Collect mohair, cotton, or wool blankets in pretty patterns, textures, and colors. Beautiful throws and blankets add texture, charm, and security wherever they are. Use them throughout your home — draped over a sofa or chair, folded at the end of a bed, or stacked on a bench. Keep them within easy reach for a touch of cozy comfort.

Cozy up to a quilt.

Old or new, quilts are a lovely and long-lasting way to bring the color and comfort of cotton to your home year-round. Collect pretty quilts that coordinate with your decor. Use them as bed coverlets or wall hangings, fold and stack them on top of a chest, or drape one over a table and cover it with glass.

8

Roll out the rugs.

Colorful cotton rag or braided rugs soften a hard, cold floor. These rugs are comfortable, reasonably priced, and reversible. Scatter small ones in places where you stand frequently — in front of your shower, tub, or kitchen sink, and at front and back doors. Do not use rag rugs on top of carpet where they might get wet and stain the carpet. For best results, dry clean.

9

Frame your furniture.

*U*se a large dhurrie, needlepoint, or Oriental area rug to frame a cozy seated area for conversation. Lay the rug either on a hard floor surface or on top of your carpet. To cushion the rug and prevent it from slipping, place a vinyl underlay or piece of carpet padding beneath it.

10

Step on it.

When selecting carpet, think quality first, then color. Walk on it with your bare feet to be sure it is soft. For high traffic areas, choose a durable, dense pile, tight level loop or cut-and-loop carpet. Use deeper, plush piles for lower traffic areas. Buy the best padding you can afford. The quality of the padding affects the comfort and life of your carpet.

Make furniture arrangements friendly.

*C*luster furniture comfortably together for conversation. Arrange pieces as if they were speaking to one another. Much like body language, furnishings placed in close proximity produce warmth, intimacy, and emotional connection among the people in the room.

If you have a large room, consider creating two smaller sitting areas.

12

Splurge on a sofa.

A well-made, comfortable sofa will provide years of satisfying seating. Before buying a sofa, sit in it to make sure it's a fit. Seat height and depth, arm height, and cushion construction all contribute to a sofa's comfort. Though soft cushions may be more comfortable, firmer cushions will retain their shape better.

Pick a personal perch.

*P*lace a favorite, comfortable chair that suits your personality and your touch by a sunny window. It may be an overstuffed club chair, a wooden gliding rocker, or a chaise lounge. In a moment of stillness, steal away to your favorite seat to spend time alone with God.

14

Be flexible.

*F*or greater flexibility and enjoyment, consider adding casters or a swivel base to a new or reupholstered club chair. Both features will give you the freedom to swing one way to watch a roaring fire or twirl around to take part in a conversation. The slight additional cost will be well worth the added comfort and convenience.

15

Put your feet up.

Have an ottoman to raise weary legs any-where in your home. Place it on casters to allow for the flexibility of additional seating. A large ottoman can be multifunctional — use it to prop feet up, to stack with beautiful books, or to accommodate a tray for serving food and bever-ages. An ottoman should be at least one inch lower than seat height of sofa or chair.

16

Keep it convenient.

*T*ry to have some type of table within reach of every seating piece in your home. This will provide a comfortable place to set a beverage, spool of thread, book, magazine, or whatever you need to keep close at hand.

Feel your fabrics.

When selecting fabrics, choose them for their feel as well as their look. Textured fabrics such as nubby wool, soft suede, woven linen, cool cotton, elegant damask, slippery chintz, or luscious velvet add interest and a pleasant touch to any upholstered furniture. The more textured and heavy a fabric, the more durable it is apt to be.

18

Go naturelle!

For a casual look, use natural fibers like sisal or sea grass rugs. With their neutral-colored, textured weave, these practical rugs subtly enhance any room that has hard surface

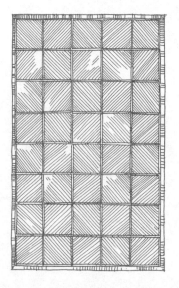

flooring. Before buying, walk on rugs in your bare feet — some are more comfortable than others. For color, use a contrast binding on the edge of a rug or stencil a pattern.

Toss in a touch of texture.

*C*ollect pretty needlepoint pillows and toss one in with a mixture of other pillows on a sofa, chair, bed, or bench. Pull out a few Christmas needlepoint pillows every year around the holidays to help decorate your home.

20

Have happy hands.

*I*f you enjoy cross-stitching, knitting, or needlepoint, or simply need to stitch on a button now and then, a pretty sewing basket will make the job a joy. Fill your sewing basket with thread, yarn, needles, pins, sharp scissors, and a thimble. Keep it close at hand for whenever you have the itch to sit and work with your hands.

Find natural finishes.

*F*or an extra touch of charm and warmth, bring God's beauty into you home by using a variety of natural finishes. Consider wicker, wood, marble, stone, slate, brick, or granite.

22

Pile on the pillows.

$\mathcal{S}$oft, squishy throw pillows come in many sizes and shapes, but all lend a touch of comfort to any corner of your home. Back beds, benches, sofas, or chairs with plump pillows. For extra-cushy comfort, use pillows filled with down — the comfortable filling will conform to your body for a cozy, satisfying backrest.

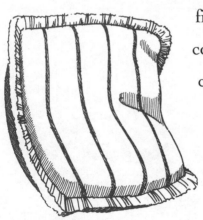

Plop onto floor pillows.

$\mathcal{K}$eep two or three jumbo pillows stacked on the floor in your living room, playroom, or children's bedroom. They provide flexible seating and serve as a great support for someone who wants to sit on the floor to watch a movie or lounge in front of a roaring fire. Floor pillows are inexpensive compared to other seating, and with zippered coverings, they can be easily cleaned.

24

Texturize your home.

*F*ill your home with a variety of textured elements, such as an iron drapery rod, a woven wicker chair, or a carved clay sculpture. Bring texture and interest to damaged or ordinary walls by mixing sand with paint.

Enjoy the feel of a fan.

*I*nstall a ceiling fan to bring a breeze to any room. Use the small switch on your fan's axis to turn blades clockwise to stay cool in warm weather and counterclockwise to circulate heat in cold weather. A ceiling fan is more attractive and safer than most portable fans. Installing an attic fan will help circulate air in a two-story home.

26

Own a cuddly companion.

*A*dopt a dog, cat, or other cuddly animal that likes to be held. The loving touch you give your pet will bring both of you loads of pleasure. If you live alone, a pet makes a comforting companion.

Don't make dusting a drag.

Throw out those skimpy scraps of old T-shirts and tattered towels for dusting. Instead, buy a dozen cotton fabric diapers for dusting. Store them in a pretty basket, and wash them after each use. Use an ostrich feather duster with a long handle for hard-to-reach places. Make time spent dusting a time to thank God for all his blessings.

28

Open up.

*B*ring the wonderful feel of the outdoors inside by opening your windows on a pleasant day and enjoying the fresh, soothing breeze as it flows through your home and touches your skin.

Polish with pleasure.

$\mathcal{E}$njoy the act of polishing brass, glass, silver, or wood. Rubbing favorite objects and restoring their natural beauty can give a great sense of satisfaction.

30

Unveil your mail.

*M*ake opening your mail a pleasant ritual with a pretty letter opener. Not only will it add beauty to the task, it will spare your hands and nails.

Make paperwork pretty.

$\mathscr{F}$ind a lovely way to display paperwork that
needs your attention. Use a brass letter rack,
silver toast caddy, or basket for filing bills
and correspondence and responding
to invitations. Keeping invitations will remind you to
write a thank-you note
as soon as you have
attended an event.

32

File with finesse.

$\mathcal{M}$ake your file system a pleasant place of touch by organizing it efficiently. For easy reference, color coordinate your file folders according to different topics: personal, business, household, et cetera.

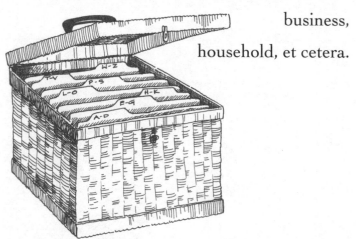

Write away.

*F*ill a pretty, compartmented basket with your favorite stationery, note cards, postcards, stamps, updated address book, labels, and a nice pen. The more convenient writing is, the more likely you are to keep in touch. Minister to others from your home through the mail.

34

Strike one!

*M*ake a hobby of collecting matches from restaurants, hotels, and other places you visit; you'll bring back memories every time you use one. Keep matchbooks in a convenient spot (out of reach of little ones) so they're handy when you need one. In the winter, keep tall wood matches in a wood box on your fireplace mantle. Or try a flame igniter, available in most hardware stores. It lights with an easy flick of the finger.

Tickle your tongue.

What type of ice do you prefer in cold beverages: crushed, small cubes, or large cubes? If you don't have an ice maker that produces your favorite ice, buy trays that will make them or purchase bags of the ice you prefer and store them in the freezer.

36

Buy the best.

*D*on't skimp on the quality of paper towels, toilet tissue, or facial tissue you use in your home. Find a brand you love for its touch, and stick with it. The better quality the paper product, the less you will need. Use coupons, and stock up when your paper items go on sale. By purchasing extra-large rolls, you will save time and energy replacing them.

Open with ease.

*C*an opening need not be a chore. Have a quality manual or electric can opener that is dependable and works with ease. If you prefer electric, try an under-the-counter model to save on counter-top clutter.

38

Keep it cozy.

*U*se a tea cozy or tea towel around your teapot to keep your beverage warm. Transfer freshly brewed coffee to an airtight thermal carafe to keep it hot for several hours.

Grab your garbage.

*L*ine a large decorative trash can in your kitchen with a sturdy garbage bag that holds well and has a built-in drawstring. For a quick trick, store additional plastic bags in the bottom of your trash can. No more fumbling to find those ties, twisties, or replace-ment bags.

40

Take a number.

*K*eep a handy basket next to the kitchen telephone with a pen and notepad to jot down messages and reminders. Use the spot for your home's communication center. Always leave a note if you must leave home before someone else is expected to arrive; it's courteous, thoughtful, and will give a sense of security to anyone entering an empty home.

Add just a pinch.

*K*eep a small dish of salt by your stove in the kitchen. When your food needs a touch of salt, use your fingers to add just a pinch. Using your fingers will allow you to have greater control over the amount of salt used while cooking or preparing food than you would if using a salt shaker.

Keep it crispy.

Wrap chips, cereals, and crackers well to prevent moisture from causing them to go stale. Use clothespins, large paper clips, or plastic clips to secure folded bags. Or store crispy foods in your pantry in clear plastic containers.

Soften your spread.

Spreading a hard chuck of butter on a piece of warm toast or fresh bread can be one of life's little hang-ups. To keep it soft and spreadable, leave butter or margarine out on the counter or kitchen table in a covered butter dish.

44

Keep your touch tender.

Wearing rubber gloves can spare your hands while washing dishes, or when opening tight lids on glass jars. Apply hand lotion to your hands from a decorative dispenser by your kitchen sink. Massaging your hands with lotion can be a small reward of touch after kitchen cleanup.

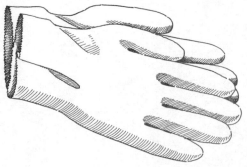

Cut it with a knife.

Sharpen knives and scissors when dull. A sharp tool makes cutting a pleasure and saves time. If you don't have a knife or scissors sharpener, many hardware stores offer professional sharpening. Protect your countertops by always cutting on a sturdy cutting board. Have a sharp pair of sewing scissors specially designated for cutting fabrics only.

46

Know your knives.

A large, wide chef's knife minces, chops, and slices fruits and vegetables. A narrower, long, slicing knife with a smooth-edged blade cuts thin, even slices of meats, vegetables, and cheeses. A serrated-edge saws breads and cakes. Use a paring knife for most small cutting jobs, and a medium-size utility knife to peel, slice, and chop.

Carve up a feast.

$\mathcal{H}$ave an excellent carving knife and serving fork. For effortless carving, use a sharp electric knife. Carving a roast or turkey should be part of a celebration, not a frustration.

48

Collect spoons in all shapes and sizes.

Smooth wooden spoons make stirring, sautéing, or tossing food a delight. Collect a variety of them and store them in a decorative canister within easy reach of the stove.

Get a grip.

*T*ransform a door or cabinet by replacing its hardware with beautiful, functional knobs or handles that feel wonderful to your grasp.

50

Hold onto hot pots.

Treat yourself to a few new pot holders when the old ones begin to look tired and tattered. A fresh new set of holders will cost very little, yet will add joy to your cooking every time you put them on to pick up something hot.

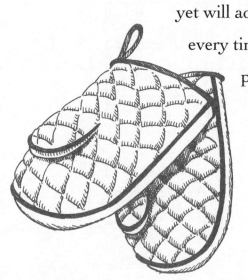

Make a splash with dish towels.

$\mathcal{R}$eplace kitchen dish towels when they become stained and dingy. Drape a pretty, all-cotton, absorbent dish towel over a kitchen cabinet door in front of your sink or thread one through your refrigera-tor door handle to wipe wet hands and dry dishes.

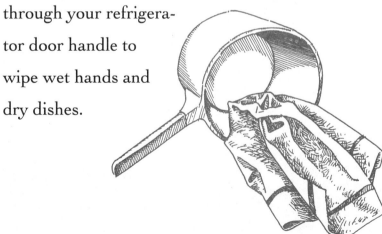

52

Tie your apron strings.

A pretty apron will add pleasure to a mundane chore, helping you prepare your heart and mind for your task, and changing what might be considered a burden into a blessing.

For a touch of casual comfort, hang a few aprons that coordinate with your kitchen colors on the pegs of a Shaker rack and place the rack in a prominent spot in your kitchen.

53

Create a window of opportunity.

*F*or comfort and coziness, transform a beautiful bay window into a functional window seat. Add hinges to the lid of your window seat to allow you to use the space below for storage. Make a seat cushion and pile on the pillows to make it a favorite perch for reading, eating, or just daydreaming.

54

Reach out and touch.

*H*old hands while praying at mealtime or any time. Give hands an extra "I love you" squeeze at the end of the prayer. The simple act of hand-holding can knit hearts and lives together.

55

Fold with a flair.

To enhance a pretty place setting, add some flair to your napkin folding. Use napkin rings, wired ribbon, raffia, clothespins, or a self-knotted bow. Thread a napkin through a teacup handle. Stuff a fluffy napkin in a stemmed glass. Buy a book on napkin folding and learn a few new, simple folds. Life is more fun when it's full of surprises!

56

Try terry cloth.

$\mathcal{S}$mall, fringed terry-cloth hand towels
work great as informal, absorbent napkins.
Keep a good supply on hand and use them
every day. They're economical, easy to care
for, comfortable to the touch, and great for
messy finger foods.

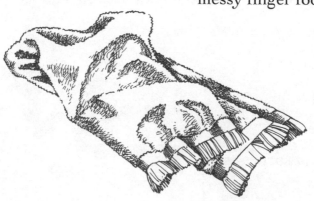

Help yourself.

*R*ather than set the table for a casual buffet with friends and family, let everyone help themselves from a utensil-holding basket caddy. Add creative flair by displaying silverware and napkin bundles in a decorative accessory like a ceramic vase or a teapot without a lid.

58

Clean up with class.

*P*rovide clean, dry hand towels and warm water with a slice of lemon, or rolled damp hand towels that have been heated in the microwave. After a messy meal of finger foods, serve them to your family and friends for a cleanup fit for royalty.

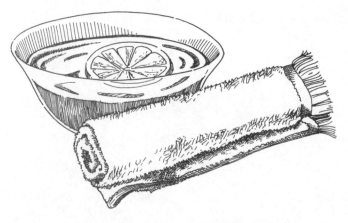

Bring a little luxury
to your lips.

Using an appropriate glass for your beverage will enhance your touch and sipping satisfaction. Try a stemmed glass for fruit juice. A mason jar for iced tea. A chunky mug for coffee. A delicate cup for hot tea. Spoil those you love — as well as yourself — when serving a beverage by offering a small, pretty paper napkin or a coaster.

60

Turn on the temperature.

*W*hen it's hot, it's hot. When it's not, it's not. Complement the temperature of food items being served. Heat glass plates or bowls in a warm oven for hot foods. Chill plates, bowls, or glasses in the freezer for serving cold items.

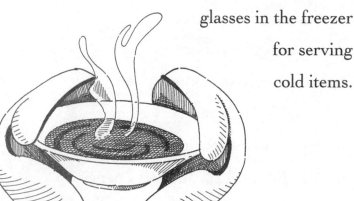

Soften your seat.

*B*uy or make pretty seat cushions for wood chairs. Add ties, tassels, or tufting to bring a little touch of beauty and comfort to seat cushions. To prevent chair pads from slipping and sliding when you sit on them, cut pieces of inexpensive vinyl rug grip and place them beneath the pad. Bring a touch of comfort to your bathroom with a cushioned toilet seat.

62

Protect with place mats.

Select place mats to protect your dining table that are both pretty and pleasing to the touch. Try natural woven mats for a casual look, or use easy-to-wipe-clean vinyl mats if you have children.

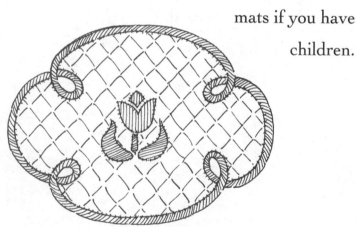

Robe yourself
in comfort.

*T*here's nothing more comfortable than wrapping yourself up in a plush terry cloth or cozy chenille bathrobe. Pick crisp, clean white or a color that looks pretty in your home. Keep your robe handy on a big hook behind your bathroom door.

64

Feel pretty as a princess.

*G*et rid of old pajamas and keep just a few, pretty comfortable pieces of nightwear in fabrics like cotton, silk, flannel, rayon, or satin. Natural fabrics allow your skin to breathe, providing a more comfortable, healthful sleep.

65

Hold on.

A hold is a hug that hangs on. Sometimes a warm embrace provides more help and healing than any wise advice or wonder drug. Try to sense when the situation calls for you to zip your lip and reach out your arms to hold a loved one.

66

Lounge around.

*P*itch the pitiful sweatpants and purchase at least one comfortable, attractive outfit that you can pull on when lounging around your home. You need not sacrifice beauty to be casual and comfortable. Of all places you should want to be attractive, it's in your private world with your loved ones.

Check it out.

*P*lace an outdoor thermometer outside your
bedroom window. Check the temperature in
the morning as you dress
for the day.

68

Drape it.

Use a quilt rack as a caddy for coverlets, comforters, or bedspreads when they're not covering your bed. This will help keep them clean and fluffy and ensure they last longer.

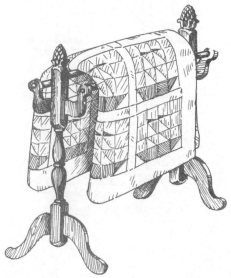

Up with down.

*I*nvest in a down duvet when they go on sale. A duvet is cool in the summer and warm in the winter and makes bed-making a breeze. With no top sheet or heavy blankets to wrestle, all you do is fluff and smooth! Place a duvet at the foot of a bed within reach for cozy comfort.

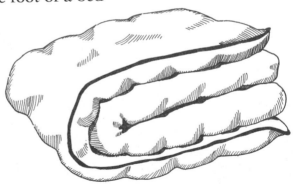

70

Get a good night's sleep.

Because we spend one-third of our lives in bed, a quality mattress is the wisest investment of material touch you can bring to your home. Flip your mattress every month to ensure it stays comfortable, wears better, and lasts longer. For maximum comfort and durability, purchase box springs and mattress as a set.

Cover up.

*P*rotect mattresses and pillows with good quality covers. Buy mattress pads that fit well, and use a zippered pillow cover before slipping on a pillowcase. For a clean, tailored look, forego a bed skirt and cover your box springs with a fitted sheet to display a beautiful bed frame.

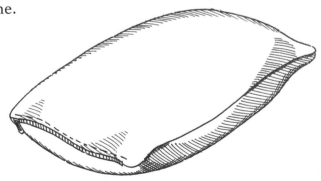

72

Satisfy with sheets.

Envelope your mattress in bedsheets that are beautiful, comfortable, and suitable to your personal preference for touch. Cool cotton sheets soothe in the summer. Cozy flannel sheets warm in the winter. Silky, satin sheets provide a little luxury anytime.

Find a cozy corner.

$\mathscr{D}$esignate a special spot in your home that is cozy, comfortable, and well-lighted as your place to be alone with God. The more convenient and comfortable it is, the more likely you will find yourself there. Keep your Bible, devotional book, and journal within easy reach.

74

Rest in peace.

*I*f time allows, and your body is craving it, take a short, guilt-free nap. There is a vast difference between laziness and rest. When you are weary, you need to rest. If you are overly tired, you'll become irritable and your perspective on life will become distorted. Refresh yourself and your outlook with adequate rest.

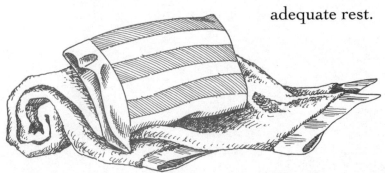

Pick a pillow.

$\mathcal{B}$e picky about your bed pillows. Treat yourself to a favorite type and size, whether it be down, feathers, polyfill, or foam filling, king, queen, or standard size. Surround yourself with pillows that provide maximum comfort. Let each family member choose the pillow type he or she prefers.

76

Prop yourself with a pillow.

*U*se a decorative pillow with arms and a firm back to prop you up while sitting in bed. Or, for lower back support, tuck a neck roll pillow behind several stacked bed pillows. A pillow prop will become a favorite item for reading, writing, or watching television in the privacy and comfort of your bedroom.

Touch a heart.

*F*or a touch of thoughtfulness, occasionally leave little sticky notes around your home for those you love. Put them where they're sure to be discovered — a mirror, phone receiver, bed pillow, or in a favorite shoe.

It's a simple gesture that will touch their hearts, put a smile on their faces, and remind them they are loved.

78

Create a comfort zone.

*Y*our bedroom should be your most private comfort zone, a place to sit, read, and enjoy a morning cup of coffee or a midnight snack. If possible, create a small sitting area in your bedroom that includes a love seat or two chairs and a tea table. If space is tight, consider a chaise lounge and a small table.

Jot in a journal.

*K*eep in touch with your own personal thoughts and prayers by writing in a journal as often as you can; it helps clear your mind of clutter, allows you to see patterns in your life, and shows you God's faithful hand in unraveling life's challenges.

80

Scrub a dub dub.

*P*our liquid body soap onto a soft mesh
puff and scrub all over your body. The
bubbling lather and tingling touch
will invigorate you!

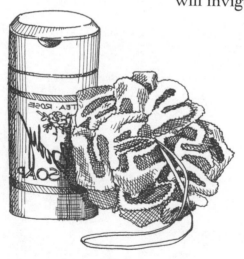

81

Touch toes.

Take time to snuggle, cuddle, and touch toes with your mate or children. Make Saturday morning a time for everyone to pile in bed (pets too!) and get close.

82

Supply a soothing touch.

*K*eep your bathroom stocked with supplies for first aid and aches and pains. Be sure to have a heating pad, hot water bottle, and soothing ointment on hand. Bring comfort and loads of love to a loved one by giving a gentle rub to an aching limb, neck, or back. A small drop of baby oil will help your hands glide over weary muscles.

Save it for a rainy day.

*F*or an effortless way to save toward something special for your home, keep a pretty jar on your bedroom dresser to store loose change from your purse or pockets.

84

Keep closets clutter-free.

*M*ake putting on your clothes a pleasure by cleaning out your closet and drawers. Sort through your wardrobe every spring and fall. Lay all your clothes out on your bed, then try each garment on. If it fits and you wear it, keep it. If it needs mending or altering, fix it. If you haven't worn it in a year, give it away and allow someone else to enjoy it.

Keep current addresses handy.

To avoid having to replace an address book, use a decorative recipe file box. Write names and addresses of friends and relatives on individual index cards and file the cards alphabetically. When an address changes, simply pull the card and replace it with an updated one.

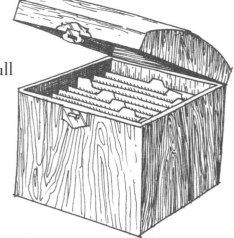

86

Bathe in bliss.

*D*raw up a warm bath for yourself or a loved one to soothe and relax before a good night's sleep. Add foaming bubble bath to tickle your body as you soak. Use a plastic bath air pillow to rest your head while soaking in the tub.

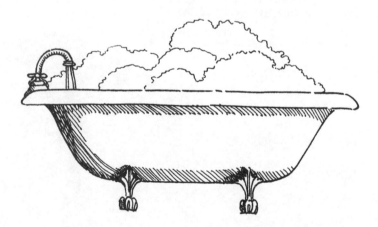

Collect touches
for the tub.

$\mathcal{K}$eep all of the necessary ingredients for a wonderful bath at your fingertips. Fill a basket next to the tub with your favorite soaps, bath salts, lotions, powders, sponges, and brushes.

88

Step safely.

$\mathcal{U}$se plush, absorbent cotton rugs to soak up slippery splashes outside your shower or tub and keep your feet safe and comfortable. They are reversible, machine washable, and available in a rainbow of colors.

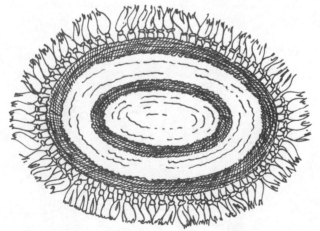

Pamper with a powder puff.

Apply a favorite perfumed powder all over your body with a big, fluffy duster. Use the powder puff on young children after a bath. They'll treasure its touch as it tickles their bodies from head to toe.

90

Store tiny touches.

Store cotton swabs and soft, fluffy cotton balls in pretty decorative canisters on a bathroom shelf — they'll be close at hand for a tiny touch to clean your body. For a colorful touch, buy pastel cotton swabs and balls that coordinate with your bathroom decor.

Have healthy hands.

*K*eep a decorative dispenser of liquid soap by every sink in your home to remind you and your family to wash your hands frequently. This simple habit can help keep your household healthy by preventing the spread of germs which lead to sickness.

92

Lather up.

*D*iscover a soap that you love, not just for its fragrance, but for its shape in your hand and the lather it makes. Enjoy the clean sensation as you lather your whole body in it. Rinse with warm water.

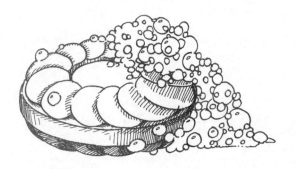

Baby your body.

*F*ind a face and body lotion that has a pleasing texture and soothes the skin. Display it in a decorative squirt dispenser, or store it out of sight when not in use. Apply frequently for a soft touch and a fresh, healthy glow. Treasure the time of touch as you care for your body. After all, it is God's temple!

94

Add a tingling touch.

*F*or a revitalizing tingle, add an adjustable
massage attachment to your showerhead.
Adjust the massage control to pulsate the
water pressure. The greater the water
pressure, the more invigorating
your shower will be.

95

Lighten your load.

Have separate laundry baskets for light and dark clothes to avoid having to sort later. Set aside specific times of the week to do laundry. This will help you work smarter, not harder, and will eliminate needless energy and stress. Pray as you fold laundry, thanking God for each loved one he's brought into your life.

96

Wrap yourself in love.

*R*oll up plush terry-cloth towels and put them in a pretty basket or stack them neatly on a small chair or wicker table by the tub. Fold or roll several small terry-cloth hand towels in a basket by the sink for drying hands and face. For a fresh-out-of-the-dryer feel, buy a towel-warming rack. After a shower or bath, wrap yourself in a big, warm, terry-cloth towel.

Weigh in.

*K*eep an accurate scale in your bathroom or closet. Place it on a sturdy, solid surface when you weigh yourself. Maintaining a healthy body weight affects your attitude and energy level, both of which affect your home's atmosphere.

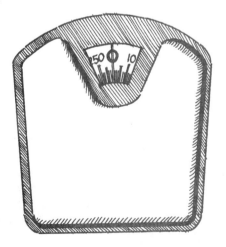

98

Dig in!

When planting flowers, vegetables, or greenery, put on a pair of gardening gloves and dig down deep into the dirt. Using your hands to nurture God's rich soil can be therapeutic. Proper soil preparation is essential for healthy growing plants, so mix nutrient-filled mulch into loose soil before planting.

Welcome with wonderful touches.

Help overnight visitors feel at home with thoughtful touches of comfort like fresh towels, a bed of pretty linens, lots of plump pillows, and a cozy blanket or quilt.

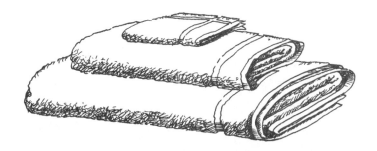

100

Secure your safety.

*F*or peace of mind, make sure you have sturdy locks on all windows and exterior doors. Ideally, all exterior doors should have dead-bolt locks. Keep a key to each dead bolt inside and close at hand, but not in the lock. Or, install a dead bolt that opens with the turn of a knob instead of a key.

101

Stay in touch with the Master.

Keep in touch with God by carving out quiet time in your day to spend reading your Bible, writing in a journal, and praying. Getting in touch with the heart of your heavenly Father will help you keep proper perspective on your life. As he brings balance to your day, gentle touches of love will no doubt be a part of the blessing you bring to your home.

101 Quick Tips
To Make Your Home
❧ Taste ❧
SenseSational

For he satisfies the thirsty and fills

the hungry with good things.

Psalm 107:9

Introduction

—❖—

God has blessed us with bountiful food and drink to nourish our bodies and satisfy our taste buds. In the same way, we can bless our family, friends, and ourselves by preparing healthy, delicious food and beverages in our homes.

God has given us almost ten thousand taste buds. Every taste of the food he has created for us gives us the chance to relish something delectable. Yet with the busyness of life, it seems we seldom slow down to savor the flavors of food and enjoy them with grateful hearts.

May the following tips inspire you to fill your home with life and love as you fill it with God's abundant bounty. Keep in mind, some of the most pleasing foods and drinks are also the most simple. Have fun tantalizing the taste buds in your home!

terry.

101 Quick Tips
To Make Your Home
❦ TASTE ❧
SenseSational

Celebrate his bounty.

God has blessed us with an abundance of delicious natural foods to strengthen, sustain, and satisfy. The vast variety of colors, textures, shapes, and flavors of food demonstrate his goodness to us. Honor God and your family by filling your home and your body with healthy, tasty foods he has created.

2

Put function first.

Organize your kitchen so that it is a comfortable and enjoyable place in which to cook and prepare food. Keep quality kitchen equipment and utensils that make kitchen tasks easier, and give away unneeded items. Arrange cabinet and drawer contents in a way that is convenient for tasks carried out nearby.

Live and learn.

When we stop learning, we stop living. Plan to become a better cook each year. Ask God to help make cooking a fun and interesting job for you. Learn more about nutrition. Take a cooking course with a friend. Try at least one new recipe a month to help cultivate new tastes.

4

Eat a variety of foods.

*H*aving a variety of foods to choose from makes it more interesting to cook, serve, and eat. Variety also contributes to a sense of satisfaction that prevents overeating. And eating different, delicious, healthy foods assures our bodies get the nutrients they need. Plan a variety of menus, using cookbooks and magazines for inspiration.

Satisfy simply.

*K*eep foods and menus simple —
they will be healthier, and you will be better
able to enjoy the food's natural flavor. Usually,
the fewer ingredients a recipe or menu has, the
cheaper and easier it will be to prepare. A
healthy piece of meat, a salad, and a whole-
grain bread make a superb simple meal.

6

Get ready for market.

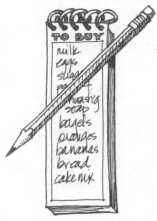

*K*eep an ongoing grocery list in your kitchen. Jot down items on the list when they get low or as family members make food requests. To keep shelves well-stocked and to prevent being caught without a needed staple, double-check your refrigerator and pantry before going to the grocery store.

Plan your menus.

*Y*ou will waste less food and save time and money while shopping if you plan your menus in advance. Plan meals that are quick to prepare or can be served more than once. Hang a list in your kitchen of menu options, crossing menus off after they have been served.

8

Shop wisely.

*B*e a wise steward with your food funds.
Clip coupons. Skim the Sunday newspaper
for special prices on grocery items. Stock up
on nonperishable items when they are on
sale. Eat a snack or meal before shopping
to prevent overbuying.

Get back to basics.

When planning meals and shopping, keep in mind the four basic food groups and daily servings needed for healthy eating: 2–3 servings of milk/dairy products; 3–5 servings of vegetables; 2–4 servings of fruit; 6–11 servings of bread, cereal, rice, and pasta; 2–3 servings of beef, poultry, fish, eggs, and beans.

10

Stock up on healthy foods.

When we eat properly, we feel and look our best — it's how God designed our bodies to work. Make the most of the life he has given you by eating healthy. The closer foods are to their natural source, the better they are for you. Stock up on healthy foods so that when hunger hits, you'll reach for the right things.

Begin with breakfast.

Starting your day out with breakfast will jump-start your digestive system into working efficiently throughout the day. It can be as simple as a glass of fresh fruit juice and a banana, a muffin, a bagel, or yogurt topped with granola.

12

Find the freshest.

When preparing foods, start with the freshest ingredients possible. This assures the best flavor and most nutritious content. Find a local farmer's market or produce stand and frequent it for fresh, seasonal produce. Avoid produce in plastic wrap; it will most likely not have as much flavor.

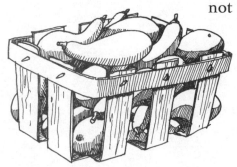

Relish your refrigerator.

$\mathcal{D}$isplay foods attractively inside your refrigerator. Use clear glass or plastic food containers to store foods. Place fruits and vegetables in bowls. Enclose meats and cheeses in clear plastic bags. Food that is out of sight is out of mind, and will probably spoil before it's remembered.

14

Celebrate the seasons.

$\mathcal{F}$or the fullest flavors, serve food and beverages that celebrate each season's bounty. To know what is in season, look for what is plentiful, healthy looking, and reasonably priced. Cool months call for hot apple cider, pot roast, citrus fruits, or vegetable soup. Warmer months welcome fresh lemonade, corn on the cob, melons, or sliced tomatoes.

15

Keep recipes current.

*C*lean out recipes you won't ever use, and plan to try those you keep. Collect good and easy recipes from outstanding cooks you know. Have a few favorite cookbooks with healthy, quick recipes. Mark recipes that are winners. Browse through a cook-book in bed at night for cooking inspiration.

16

Share a specialty.

*F*ind a food you enjoy cooking, and make
it your trademark dish: homemade breads,
cookies, soups, salads — whatever comes
easy and is enjoyable to you. Share your
specialty with others.

Let little hands help.

$\mathcal{T}$hough letting children help with the cooking may not be the fastest method, your efforts may bear rich fruit. Children are more apt to experiment with eating if they have helped in preparation, and cooking together allows you to talk with them while they help.

18

Freeze it!

*F*reezing is one of the best ways to preserve flavor, but even frozen food doesn't last forever. Store foods in moisture-proof packaging like plastic containers, freezer bags, or heavy foil. Mark contents and the date frozen clearly on packages. Eat cooked frozen foods within six weeks to assure freshest flavor.

Triple the taste.

*C*ook a triple batch of a recipe. Eat one, freeze one, and share one with a family or neighbor in need of encouragement. You will not only get two great meals for your family, you'll feel the joy of sharing! (If you have children, let them help deliver the food, so they can learn the joy of sharing too!)

20

Go with garlic.

Garlic gives great flavor to foods. To prevent them from drying out, skin cloves and refrigerate them in a jar of olive oil. You can use cloves as needed for garlic-flavored cooking oil or salad dressing. Prepeeled or minced garlic is available in most grocery stores. For a great garlic taste, rub a prepeeled clove inside a wooden salad bowl before adding greens.

Pep it up with pepper.

*P*epper adds spice, texture, and eye appeal to almost any food. It loses its potent flavor soon after it is ground, so for the fullest flavor, grind your own fresh peppercorns with a pepper mill. Try crushing peppercorns in a paper bag to coat steaks, a roast, or fish before cooking. Or simmer whole pep-percorns in slow-cooking dishes.

22

Make it better with butter.

*B*utter always adds a burst of rich flavor. For a terrific taste, flavor butter by sprinkling jalapeno, onion, black pepper, basil, and parsley onto a stick of softened butter. Mix all the ingredients together, roll them into a log, wrap, and freeze for use on broiled meats and fish or to stir into vegetables or pastas. You can also mix fruit preserves and a touch of confectioners' sugar with softened butter for fresh breads.

Flavor with fresh herbs.

*F*resh herbs, available in most grocery produce sections, help accent the natural flavor of any food. Try using fresh herbs for garnishes or in salads. Mix whole leaves of basil, cilantro, or mint with salad greens. (Dried herbs are much more potent in flavor than fresh herbs, so use one-third as much dried herbs than fresh when cooking.)

24

Vary your vinegars.

Vinegars give vitality to many dishes, with few calories and no fat. They come in a variety of flavors and colors. Tantalize your taste buds by experimenting with different ones. For a somewhat sweet flavor, try rice or raspberry vinegar in green salads with fruit. For a tangy taste, use tarragon, balsamic, or red wine vinegar in salads with vegetables.

Dress up your salad.

*M*ake sure greens are dry before dressing a salad. Test different dressings and oils for flavor. For a tasty dressing, add Dijon mustard to oil and vinegar. Or for a citrus zing, replace vinegar with the juice of a freshly squeezed lemon, lime, or orange. A dressing should enhance the salad's flavor, not overpower it. After mixing a dressing, toss it well and taste it before serving.

26

Choose the "cream of the crop."

*F*or maximum freshness and vitamin content, choose vegetables with rich, bright colors that are firm to the touch: the darker and richer the color, the greater the nutrients. Smaller vegetables often have a more tender texture and more flavor. Steam fresh vegetables lightly in water with lemon juice to keep nutrients and vibrant color.

Consider carrots.

*C*arrots are a versatile kitchen staple, available year-round. Buy a bag of prepeeled, miniature carrots to have on hand for a ready-to-eat, healthy, crunchy snack. Add chopped carrots to soups, stews, and tomato sauce for a natural and nutritious sweet flavor. For a superb side dish, lightly sauté carrots in butter, brown sugar, orange juice, and basil.

28

Serve artichokes as appetizers.

$\mathcal{S}$pring is prime time for artichokes. Purchase artichokes that are heavy and have tightly closed leaves. To keep their vibrant color, steam them in water with lemon juice. The artichoke is ready when its cooked leaves

lift easily from its base. Dip artichoke leaves and heart in lemon butter or mayonnaise mixed with parmesan cheese.

Pile on the potatoes.

The potato is the most consumed vegetable in America today. Be creative with this economical vegetable. Serve potatoes hot or cold, as a side dish, in a salad, or as a main dish. Load a baked potato with fresh vegetables for a healthy meal. Celebrate spring with new potatoes steamed in butter and black pepper, and tossed in fresh dill.

30

Scoop it out.

A natural serving container makes a creative edible dish for delicious foods. Hollow out a loaf of bread or a small cabbage head for vegetable dips. Fill a large beefsteak tomato with chicken, tuna, or shrimp salad. Stuff and cook a green pepper with ground beef and rice.

On with the onions!

&xperiment with different flavored onions. Add leeks to soup broth for a mild, somewhat sweet taste. Use fresh, frozen, or dried chives in baked potatoes and egg or seafood dishes to bring color and a delicate onion flavor. Slice red onions to enhance salads and sandwiches. Bake sweet onions, like Vidalias, whole in butter for a tasty side dish. Try raw scallions in dip.

32

Tempt with tomatoes.

Take advantage of tasty tomatoes in the summer. Eat a plum tomato whole like an apple, slice it for sandwiches, or puree it for sauce. Serve sliced beefsteak tomatoes with chopped parsley for a simple summer vegetable. Lightly sauté cherry tomatoes in olive oil and season them to taste with fresh ground pepper and salt. To assure the fullest flavor, avoid using tomatoes out of season.

33

Cool off with cucumbers.

*F*or a cool summer side dish, marinate cucumber slices and red onions in cider vinegar, water, salt, and pepper. For a healthy snack, munch on crunchy, raw pickling cucumbers.

34

Satisfy with squash.

Enjoy the succulent tastes of seasonal squash. In the fall and winter, slice acorn squash in half, remove seeds and steam it with butter, brown sugar, and cracked peppercorns. In the spring and summer, stir fry, steam, or grill yellow crookneck and green zucchini squash. As an exquisite side dish, sauté miniature squash in butter and spices. Or eat squash raw with dips.

Munch on mushrooms.

Mushrooms are good all year long in salads, egg dishes, or sauces. Sauté whole or sliced mushrooms in burgundy or white cooking wine for a delicious topping for beef, poultry, or fish or as a side dish. Fill hollowed-out mushroom caps with chopped spinach, garlic, and grated Parmesan cheese. Broil the caps until the filling is slightly crunchy. Serve as an appetizer or side dish.

36

Bring on the berries!

Enjoy delicious berries when in season. Luscious berries should be plump, vibrantly colored, and unblemished. Avoid overripe berries that are leaking juice and strawberries with brown leaves. Serve berries plain, with a touch of cream or whipped cream, in salads or cereals. For a healthy, all-fruit spread, try berry preserves on toast, bagels, or croissants.

Freeze fruit.

*F*reeze fresh seedless grapes for a cold, sweet snack. Enjoy all-natural frozen fruit juice bars in raspberry, strawberry, or grape. You can make your own by freezing fresh fruit juice in small paper cups. For a handle, insert a wooden popsicle stick just before the juice freezes. Peel away the cup when ready to eat.

38

Guarantee great grapes.

Gently shake a bunch of grapes before buying. Fresh, sweet grapes should cling tightly to the stem, and sour grapes often have a brown or grayish color. Eat grapes for a healthy snack or toss them into salads for color, texture, and flavor. For an easy meal, serve a bunch of grapes with a wedge of cheese and French bread.

Reach for the ripe.

*T*he ripeness of fruits such as peaches, plums, pears, and nectarines can be tested by placing them in your palm and gently squeezing them. If the fruit gives to light pressure and smells sweet and delicious, it's ready to eat. For the juiciest citrus fruits, select those that are the heaviest. To ripen fruit quickly, place it in a brown paper bag, close the bag loosely, and store it at room temperature.

40

Maximize your salads.

*S*alads are an easy, delicious way to eat more fruits and vegetables throughout the day. Keep salads healthy with low-fat ingredients like fruits and vegetables, kidney or garbanzo beans, and lean beef, poultry, or seafood.

Go for fresh greens.

Build salads with a tasty mixture of leafy greens. The darker the greens, the greater the nutrients. Combine tangy greens with those milder in flavor, crisp greens with tender varieties, and pale greens with those flashier in color. If you wash and wrap fresh greens in paper towel as soon as you get them home, they'll be convenient and clean when you want to whip up a salad.

42

Fix a quick salad.

*B*uy packages of ready-to-use spinach, lettuces, and slaw mixes; they cost only a few pennies more and are very convenient. Choose packages carefully to assure freshness. For an instant salad, cut a wedge of iceberg lettuce and drizzle on your favorite healthy dressing.

43

Go nuts!

Enhance salads with a handful of nuts or sunflower seeds. Try walnuts, pecans, almonds, or peanuts in salads, toasting them lightly to bring out their flavor. If you don't have young children in your home, place a wooden bowl filled with different sizes, shapes, and flavors of nuts in your living room. Leave a nutcracker and a pick in the bowl so family and friends can help themselves.

44

Liven up with olives.

*A*dding black olives is a fast and flavorful way to enhance many dishes like antipastos, pizzas, salads, chicken, spaghetti, and casseroles. Save time by buying them prepared as you need them — sliced, chopped, whole with pits, or pitted. Green olives are delicious in salads as well.

Try turkey.

For healthy, low-fat protein, roast a whole turkey, turkey breast, or boneless turkey breast. Gobble on it for a few days; then make turkey and rice soup. Use ground turkey instead of, or combined with, ground beef. Keep sliced deli turkey on hand for sandwiches and salads. For a fun change, try tasty turkey salami for sandwiches.

46

Bake bread.

*B*read can add sustenance, flavor, and most importantly, fiber to any meal. Breads made from whole grains are the best for our bodies. Enjoy a banana bran muffin for breakfast, a simple sandwich on whole wheat bread for lunch, or a whole grain roll with dinner.

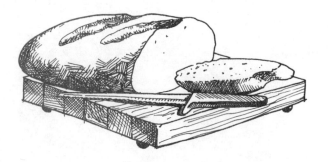

Pork out.

*P*ork and fruit are a natural pair. Simmer cutlets in your favorite jam mixed with a little vinegar or water. For a sweet and sour taste, microwave pork with pineapple and green pepper in French dressing, orange marmalade, and dry onion soup mix. For delicious, flavorful meat, grill a marinated pork roast or tenderloin.

48

Please pass the pasta!

*P*repare various sizes, shapes, colors, and flavors of pastas. Sauté fresh vegetables in garlic and olive oil and toss them in cooked pasta. Add tuna, chicken, or shrimp, if desired, and serve piping hot or chilled. For an easy seafood pasta dish, steam fresh shrimp or mussels and place them on spaghetti that's been tossed in a red clam sauce.

Simmer soups.

Learn to master at least one easy soup. Try a hot favorite, like French onion soup, in the winter, or a cool, vegetable-rich gazpacho in the summer. Buy cans of healthy soups for convenient, quick meals. For an easy and hearty meal, serve soup, salad, and fresh bread, or soup and a sandwich.

50

Go healthy with snack attacks.

*H*ave healthy snacks on hand when hunger hits. Try fresh or dried fruits, pretzels, nuts, raisins, popcorn, or vegetables cut up in cold water. Sprinkle popcorn with Parmesan cheese. Buy baked tortilla chips instead of fried, and serve with salsa. Set out a light snack when 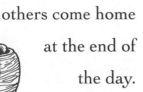 others come home at the end of the day.

Have fun with food!

*B*reak out of the mold of boring mealtimes.
Have an indoor picnic, or a make-your-own
pizza, tostada, or fajita party. Try a pasta or
potato bar. Let kids pitch in on the fun! Make
a ritual of certain meals, like celebrating the
weekend with a fun meal on Friday night or
a big breakfast on Satur-
day morning.

52

Get fancy with fruit.

Make a delightful dessert by jazzing up crepes, waffles, pancakes, pastry puffs, angel food cake, or shortcake with fresh fruit and ice cream or whipped cream. Try timesaving, ready-made crepes, cakes, frozen waffles, or pastry puffs. For an extra-tasty surprise, use strawberry or chocolate flavored whipped creams, available in most dairy departments.

Order up an omelet.

*O*melets are a quick and easy meal to serve
for breakfast, lunch, or dinner. Use the freshest
eggs and ingredients possible. For a fluffy
omelet, use eggs that are room temperature.
Toss in your favorite vegetables, cheese,
or meat for a marvelous meal
anytime.

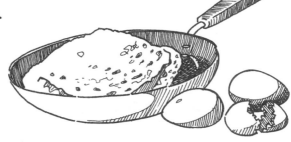

54

Say cheese.

The taste of rich cheese melts in your mouth. Serve French bread with warm Brie cheese topped with sliced almonds. Mix cream cheese with minced garlic and coarse ground pepper for a tasty spread on celery sticks or crackers. Crumble blue cheese, apple slices, and walnuts into a spinach salad. Add Feta cheese to peppers, ripe olives, and greens for a Greek salad.

Go for it!

*F*or a "too-tired-to-cook" night, pick up a healthy dinner at a specialty food shop or order in Chinese. Try to make it the exception, not the rule. Thank God for providing your meal and enjoy a night off!

56

Set the stage.

A set table sends a message of care and preparation. The most enjoyable meals are prepared simply and presented beautifully. Even if eating alone, value the life God has created in you by setting a pretty place setting for yourself. Food always tastes better when there is beauty to behold.

Calm with candlelight.

$\mathcal{L}$ight a candle when you sit down to dinner. The quiet flicker of the flame will calm you so that you eat and digest your food more slowly and linger over your meal. Eating should be an experience that causes you to not only stop and savor the tastes God has created, but to savor life itself.

58

Have a seat.

 Make it an important habit to sit when eating meals — it will affect your mind-set and your meal. Also, eat with others whenever possible. A meal shared with family or friends is ultimately a more satisfying experience. A person is more likely to eat healthy when dining with others. If you live alone, why not start a supper club and take turns cooking?

Cleanse your palette.

$\mathcal{S}$erve a small scoop of lemon or lime sherbet as a light, refreshing dessert or palette cleanser between courses. To freshen breath after meals, eat a sprig of parsley or mint. Place a jar of peppermints where you exit your home for a quick breath of freshness when walking out the door.

60

Feast your eyes on food.

*T*antalize your taste buds by serving food attractively. Think of your plate as a canvas and your food as the painting. For example, rather than toss a mixture of fruits into a bowl, arrange them beautifully as a fruit platter. When planning menus, vary color, texture, and taste for an appealing meal.

Celebrate life!

*F*or a special celebration or birthday meal, allow the person being honored to select the menu. Serve their favorite food on a "You are special today" plate or any sentimental piece of dishware. If you have china, silver, and crystal, enjoy them frequently instead of saving them for special occasions.

62

Gussy up with garnishes.

Garnishes are to food what accessories are to furniture. Observe how restaurants display foods and accent with garnishes. Fresh fruit, flowers, vegetables, and lettuce leaves all make good garnishes. You can also use fresh parsley or mint sprigs for a touch of green garnish to meals.

Cleanse your body, soul, and mind.

*C*onsider fasting to draw you closer to God in prayer and cleanse your body of impurities. While you fast, be sure to drink plenty of pure drinking water. After fasting, you will feel better, have a renewed intimacy with God, and better appreciate the simple pleasure of taste and eating.

64

Skewer it.

Skewer tasty, colorful combinations of food. On metal skewers, grill beef, shrimp, or chicken with mushrooms, onions, cherry tomatoes, and green peppers.

Create an edible centerpiece.

*F*or a beautiful and economical focal point, create an edible centerpiece. Fill a basket or bowl with colorful, seasonal, fresh fruit or vegetables. Use squash and small pumpkins in the fall, green or red apples in the winter, lemons and limes in the spring, peaches, plums, and pears in the summer.

66

Be a happy hostess.

When practicing hospitality, keep it simple and easy by preparing as much ahead of time as possible. Serve a simple casserole, salad, and bread. Food should never be more important than the people. The more relaxed you are, the more relaxed everyone will be. Preparing ahead will help you enjoy your family and friends and make your time together casual and comfortable.

Try a trifle.

*C*reate your own sweet, layered luxury. Use a large, clear glass bowl, and alternate layers of your favorite sweet treats like unfrosted cake cubes, fruit, pudding, whipped cream, and chocolate bar bits. Drizzle with a generous portion of chocolate sauce or thawed frozen strawberries in their juice. Refrigerate overnight to allow ingredients to congeal.

68

Go bananas!

*F*or a scrumptious, inexpensive dessert to warm your heart and stomach, make bananas Foster. Slice bananas lengthwise, then melt butter, brown sugar, and cinnamon and pour the mixture over the bananas. Add coconut, if desired. Sauté on the stove or bake in the oven. Serve hot on top of vanilla ice cream for a great winter dessert.

Create colossal cookies.

*U*se an ice cream scooper to portion out a batch of your favorite cookie dough. Wet your hands with water and smash the dough down into five-inch rounds on greased cookie sheets. After baking, write out a message in frosting to a loved one.

70

Toast your taste buds.

*M*ake a dessert treat that is not only tasty, but toasty too! Bake brownies and serve them while still hot topped with vanilla ice cream or yogurt. For an instant and sweet frosting for cupcakes or any baked goods, top them with marshmallows two minutes before removing the baked item from the oven.

Fix fresh fruit.

*F*resh in-season fruit is a terrific dessert alternative to heavy, sweet desserts. Dish out juicy peaches and cream, sweet chunks of watermelon with mint leaves, or succulent strawberries with tender slices of peeled kiwi.

Combine honeydew balls, blueberries, and green grapes, and toss them in lime juice with fresh mint leaves.

72

Dip it.

*F*or a fun dessert sure to tantalize the taste buds, dip fresh fruits on toothpicks into brown sugar, powdered sugar, coconut, yogurt, and caramel or fruit sauce (available in most produce sections). Enjoy apple slices covered in warm caramel sauce. Dip bananas in chocolate sauce, then in coconut. Savor strawberries dipped in vanilla yogurt, then in brown sugar.

73

Cover it.

*T*o cover strawberries, dried fruits, caramel, nuts, or pretzels with chocolate, cut up your favorite semisweet or sweet bar of chocolate or white chocolate, melting the pieces over very low heat in a small, heavy pan. Fruit must be thoroughly dried before dipping or the chocolate will not stick. Use a toothpick to hold food while dipping.

74

Scream for ice cream.

For an impressive but easy and inexpensive
dessert, layer ice cream sandwiches in a flat
pan, top with Cool Whip, then with Heath Bar
bits. Repeat layers. Freeze. Before serving,
remove from freezer, cut in squares, and drizzle
with hot fudge sauce. Your guests will never
guess how easy it was
to prepare!

Fondue for fun.

*F*or a fun, interactive way to prepare and enjoy food, serve fondue. Start with cheese fondue with breads and vegetables as an appetizer. For dinner, try cooking chicken, shrimp, or beef in peanut oil, and serve with tasty side sauces. For dessert, dip fresh fruits or cakes in warm chocolate sauce.

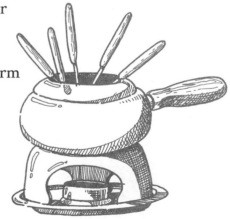

76

Eat outdoors.

*E*njoy the spectacular sights, sounds, and smells of nature by eating outdoors. When spring is in the air, serve a leisurely weekend breakfast outdoors, or sit outdoors and sip a cup of tea while you spend time with God. On a sunny afternoon, put on your bathing suit and eat a picnic lunch in your backyard. On a beautiful evening, dine by candlelight under the stars.

Grill for goodness.

*I*f you have a grill, use it often for tasty, quick meals and an easy, no pots or pans clean-up. Gas grill smoking chips bring the smoky flavors of hickory and mesquite to outdoor barbecuing. Add butter, salt, and pepper to corn on the cob, potatoes, whole onions, or squash, cover them in heavy foil, and toss them on the grill while your meat cooks.

78

Make it marvelous with marinade.

Delicious marinades add flavor and interest to grilling. Marinate salmon or tuna in teriyaki sauce and lime juice before grilling. Baste often while cooking. Tenderize a flank steak in Italian dressing before grilling. Marinate chicken in Dijon mustard or soy sauce and cook on foil on the grill. Baste shrimp or fish with lemon butter and pepper.

Feast on finger foods.

Enjoy the occasional casual pleasure of eating foods that invite you to roll up your sleeves and dig in. Serve corn on the cob, barbecue ribs, crabs, chicken, peel and eat shrimp, or wedges of watermelon. The more senses we use, the more memories we retain. Finger foods make memorable meals. The outdoors is an ideal setting for a fun finger feast.

80

Bring out the baskets.

*U*se baskets as attractive containers for serving food. Use flat baskets to hold hot casserole dishes, and baskets lined with pretty napkins to serve chips and breads. Try a small basket lined with a paper doily to hold a sandwich, fresh vegetables, and a pickle for a lunch that's quick to clean up.

Master one menu.

*I*f you don't feel confident when it comes to cooking for company, come up with one great menu you can serve whenever you have guests. Master it by making it often. Enjoy your company as they enjoy your delicious "specialty."

82

Grow a garden.

*I*f you have a sunny spot in your backyard and the slightest urge to try to grow something, dig in. Plant one little tomato or herb plant and see what happens. What do you have to lose? A little time and water may breed tasty rewards.

Offer a gracious greeting.

Offering and preparing a beverage for a family member or friend is a warm and gracious gesture that says "welcome." Keep a variety of beverages on hand to satisfy the slightest thirst. Make it a ritual to prepare a healthy, tasty beverage for yourself when you come home.

84

Drink water.

*R*etrain your taste buds to enjoy the fresh taste of pure drinking water. The more you drink, the better you'll feel! If your tap water isn't tasty and you don't have a water filter, buy drinking water. Keep a cold pitcher of it in the refrigerator, and place a small carafe of water with a glass by your bedside.

Sip some cider.

*E*njoy the sweet taste of fresh apple cider in the fall. Serve it cold or hot. For a quick and inexpensive alternative to apple cider, melt one cup of red hot cinnamon candies in one gallon of apple juice. It's a great beverage for parties or to make ahead and microwave one cup at a time.

86

Pour in the punch.

*F*or a delicious, refreshing punch that won't stain if spilled, add lemon-lime carbonated drink to white grape or apple juice. Serve over crushed ice with a mint leaf.

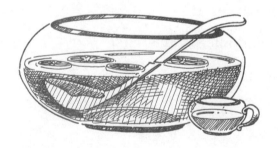

Quench your thirst.

Keep plenty of chilled, fresh fruit juices to quench the thirst of those you love. Try orange, grapefruit, apple, and grape juice, as well as many fruit combinations. For a fun afternoon with children that will teach them to enjoy serving others, set up a lemonade stand in your neighborhood. Don't charge for the lemonade. The experience will be priceless.

88

Let the sunshine in.

*M*ake iced tea the easy way — let the warm sunshine brew it! Place fresh water and tea bags in a loosely lidded glass jar and set it in the sun. Let the tea bags steep for several hours. Stir in fresh mint and sugar, if desired, and refrigerate. For a refreshing taste, add fresh orange juice or lemonade to iced tea.

Top off your hot chocolate.

Enhance a steamy mug of hot chocolate with a tasty swirl of whipped cream and a sprinkle of cinnamon sugar or chocolate shavings. At Christmas, add a candy cane stir stick. For a cool hot chocolate sundae, add a small scoop of vanilla or chocolate ice cream and top it with small marshmallows, sprinkles, and a maraschino cherry.

90

Brew a cup of coffee.

Store ground coffee and coffee beans in airtight containers. Coffee should stay fresh for two to three weeks in the refrigerator and for about two months in the freezer. Defrost beans before grinding. When brewing, start with cold water, preferably filtered drinking water. Transfer freshly-brewed coffee to an airtight, thermal carafe to keep it from tasting burnt or bitter.

Create a zesty zing.

$\mathcal{B}$ring citrus flavor to any beverage by squeezing in a lemon, lime, or orange, leaving the fruit in the glass to garnish the beverage. Add lemon or lime to water or sodas. Give hot tea a zingy twist by adding an orange peel to the teapot a few minutes before serving tea.

92

Trim the rim.

*T*here are many ways to add a beautiful touch of taste to a beverage. Stir tea, coffee, or hot chocolate with a cinnamon stick. Garnish tomato juice with a leafy stalk of celery. Add mint to lemonade or fruit juice. Slide a whole strawberry or an orange or lemon slice onto a glass rim. For a sweet luxury to the lips, wet the rim of a glass and touch it to a plate of sugar. After freezing the glass, fill it with ice and your favorite sweet beverage.

Stir in some sugar.

*D*ispense sugar cubes into your beverage with tongs, or add a small amount of sugar by using a sugar pourer with a lidded spout. For a sweet holiday treat, mix granulated sugar with colored sugar crystals.

94

Give a new twist to ice cubes.

Fill an ice tray one-third full with water or another beverage, such as lemonade or tea. Then place a mint leaf, citrus peel, raspberry, or an edible flower, like a pansy, in each compartment. When slightly frozen, fill the ice tray to the top with liquid and freeze.

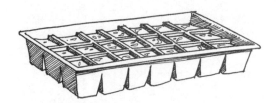

Eat where you live.

*O*ne of the easiest ways to bring variety and pleasure to the foods we eat is to change the room setting. Take advantage of cozy fires on cold winter nights, sit on the floor at your coffee table, use wicker lap trays or television trays, or eat at a card table.

96

Savor the flavor.

*S*et an atmosphere that will enhance your enjoyment of a tasty meal by turning off any distractions. The eating environment needs to be as calming as possible. If it is stressful, it will affect your digestion process and prevent you from fully enjoying the flavor of the food.

Take time for tea.

Whether alone or with a friend or family member, enjoy the simple and satisfying ritual of taking time out of your day to drink a cup of hot tea. Try several different flavored tea bags or add a touch of cream to tea for rich flavor. Keep a tin of sugar cookies on hand to eat when having tea; they store well and keep fresh. Invite neighborhood children to a dress-up tea party.

98

Treat with a little sweet.

Fill a pretty jar with special, tasty candies that coordinate with your decor. Tuck some snack-size candy bars in the freezer for an occasional sweet surprise. Or, as a real splurge in sweetness, tantalize the taste buds like the finest hotels do: Fold down the

 bedsheets of a house-guest or loved one and place a tasty bite of something sweet on their pillow.

99

Enjoy the lap of luxury.

*T*reat a loved one or yourself to a meal or snack in bed for a celebration, a sickness, or just for a taste of encouragement. Use a wicker bed tray or a serving tray. To start their school year out with an extra measure of homegrown love, serve kids breakfast in bed on their first day of class.

100

Sip yourself to sleep.

*A*fter an especially stressful day or when having difficulty sleeping, treat yourself or a loved one to a cup of hot tea in bed. Herbal tea is naturally decaffeinated, and the soothing flavor will quiet your body and mind. Try chamomile for a subtle, relaxing taste.

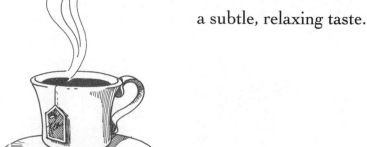

101

Taste and see that the Lord is good.

$\mathcal{C}$hrist is the true Bread of Life. While delicious food may temporarily meet our physical needs, only Jesus Christ can feed our spirits and satisfy us fully. Spend time getting to know the Savior who fully satisfies.

101 Quick Tips
To Make Your Home
❧SOUND☙
SenseSational

Better a dry crust with peace and quiet than

a house full of feasting, with strife.

Proverbs 17:1

Introduction

— ✦ —

God has given us ears as antennas to tune into the world around us, and to provide the brain with a great deal of information about our surroundings. Sound has a powerful effect on our minds, emotions, and memories. It can warn us of danger, locate things, bring pleasure or pain, and soothe or stimulate.

From the songs we play to the words we say, the choices we make about sound can intensely affect our home's atmosphere. There is perhaps no greater reflection of the condition of our hearts and our homes than the sounds which fill our walls.

May the following tips encourage you to listen carefully to the sounds in your home. Cherish those that are pleasing, eliminate those that are disturbing, and add some that are soothing. God bless you as you bring harmony to your home!

Terry.

101 QUICK TIPS
TO MAKE YOUR HOME
SOUND
SenseSational

Listen up.

$\mathcal{U}$se the ears God has given you to monitor the condition of your home and heart. Open your ears and mind to the sounds filling your home. Make every effort to enhance your home's atmosphere with pleasant sounds and to reduce those that are unpleasant and within your control to change.

2

Tune in to the outdoors.

*T*he sounds of the outside world can be the most soothing sounds to our ears. Open your windows and listen to crickets chirping, rain falling, wind whispering, thunder clapping — even the beautiful silence of a snowfall.

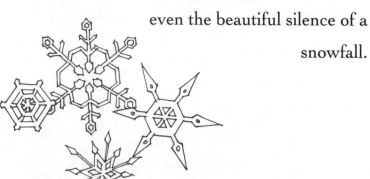

3

Come one,
come all!

*M*ount a big iron bell on a wood post outside your home as a welcoming sign of liberty and love. Ring it to round up your children from playing in the neighborhood. Or have a simple bell you can take outside and ring as a "come home" call. Once they hear it, they'll come running!

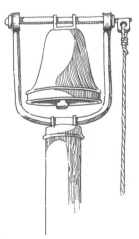

4

Cherish chirping.

Enjoy the sweet chirping of birds outside your home by placing a bird feeder or birdhouse near a kitchen window or any window that you view often. As the birds discover your friendly favor, your home will become a favorite place for them, and their singing will be music to your ears.

5

Hang charming chimes.

*H*ang a pleasant-sounding wind chime in a breezy spot on your porch, patio, or deck. It will make music with the whispering of the wind. Find a wind chime beautiful to your eyes and subtle to your ears.

6

Be friendly across fences.

*B*e a witness in the world in which God has planted you by showing love and care. Walk outside your front door and visit with your neighbors. Talk to them about what's going on in their lives. Courtesy is contagious. A friendly neighborhood starts with being a friendly neighbor.

Trickle in tranquility.

*E*njoy the gentle sound of trickling water from a small, flowing fountain as it turns your garden, patio, or sunroom into a soothing oasis. Many fountains contain pumps that recirculate the water, so no plumbing is needed.

8

Dingdong.

*D*on't overlook the ability your doorbell has for making a friendly first impression. The doorbell is usually the first sound guests will hear when visiting your home. There are many different doorbell styles, sizes, and sounds available. Choose a ring that suits your home and satisfies your ears.

Knock, knock.

*D*isplay a brass knocker on your front door that reflects your home's style. For an extra personal touch, have it engraved with your family name to welcome guests and let them know they are at the right home.

10

Tie one on.

*T*ie a lovely bell or string of bells to your entrance doorknob with a pretty piece of ribbon. The welcoming jingle will acknowledge when anyone is coming and going, and become a familiar greeting to loved ones stepping inside.

Know people's names.

$\mathcal{C}$all those visiting your home by name. The simple act of remembering others' names is a personal, caring touch that lets them know they are loved and that their lives are important. Ask your regular mail carrier, UPS deliverer, and service workers their names. Write them down and remember to address them appropriately when you see them. They'll never forget your home!

12

Shoo flies!

*T*he buzzing sound of an insect zooming through a room can drive even the calmest souls crazy. Keep a flyswatter on a hook in a handy place. Tie a pretty bow on its handle and swat away whenever necessary.

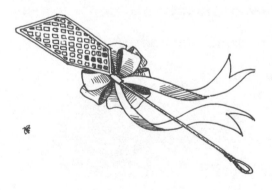

13

Arrive to instant atmosphere.

$\mathcal{S}$et your stereo on a timer to come on before you enter your home at night. Or plug your stereo system into a wall outlet wired to a light switch. Walk in and flick the switch for instant atmosphere!

14

Honk your horn.

$\mathcal{M}$ake it a family ritual that whoever drives into the garage announce his or her arrival by honking the car horn. This little sound will give your heart a lift every time you hear it, knowing a loved one has made it safely back home again. As soon as you hear the honk, head for the back door to meet the person with a warm and loving greeting.

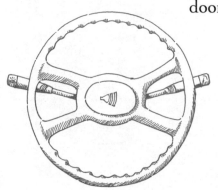

15

Set the mood with music.

When family or friends enter your home, let the music set the mood for your time together. Select music appropriate for the occasion: Play peaceful, mellow music to wind down a long, hard day; upbeat music for a fun, lively party; calm, classical music for a touch of sophistication; jazz for an easy, carefree feeling.

16

Give a wind-down welcome.

When loved ones walk in the door after a busy day, give them time to wind down before stirring up a lot of conversation. Most people need to slow down and shift gears when they get home. Respect a loved one's need for a few private moments and he or she will be more likely to speak up when the time is right.

Quiet quirky noises.

While it's true that some quirky noises give a home its unique personality, many only give their homeowners a headache. Eliminate sounds that bother you in your home. Oil squeaky doors or drawers.

Fix noisy fans.

Replace creaky

floorboards.

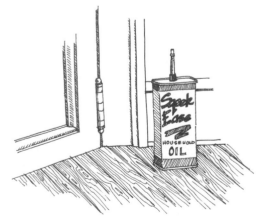

18

Express your love.

We can never hear enough of the three words "I love you." Don't miss an opportunity to let your family members know you love them. Tell them in the morning as they leave your home, in the evening before they go to sleep, on the telephone, in a note in their lunch box, or any time the emotion strikes your heart. These words of love will ring in their ears.

Sound off for safety.

*F*or maximum fire prevention safety in your home, install a smoke detector in every room that has a door that can be closed. Change the batteries annually to ensure safety. Many smoke detectors make a tiny beeping sound when their batteries need replacing.

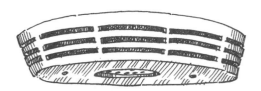

20

Wipe out whining.

Make a conscious effort to not whine or complain, and encourage your family to do the same. Constant complaining and whining signal an ungrateful heart and can drive others away or take them down with you. If you are struggling in this area, ask God to help you. Begin by thinking about and writing down your life's blessings.

Praise their presence!

*L*et others know you are genuinely glad to have them in your home by telling them so. Whether it be a child home from school or a visitor sharing a meal, they will appreciate knowing their presence matters in your home.

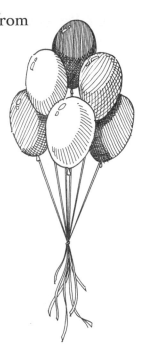

22

Hang up in a hurry.

$\mathcal{M}$ake it a habit to get off the phone as soon as you hear a loved one come home. Kindly tell whomever you are speaking with that you don't like to be on the phone when your family walks in, and that you can continue the conversation at another time. This simple gesture will let your family, as well as your friend, know your priorities, and both will be blessed because of it.

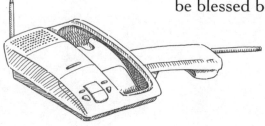

Tick, tock.

*P*lace a beautiful clock with pleasant-sounding chimes in a prominent spot in your home. Most chiming clocks strike every quarter and announce the hour with their chimes. Whether it be a classic clock resting on the fireplace mantle or a stately grandfather clock filling your entrance, the familiar sound will ring "home" every time it strikes.

24

Silence heavy machinery.

*T*ry to avoid running the dishwasher, washing machine, dryer, or any noisy machinery after your family returns home at the end of the day. Appliances can be notorious noisemakers and can add to one's stress level. This simple gesture of silencing life's conveniences allows your family to hear only pleasant, familiar sounds when coming home.

Shop, look, and listen.

When shopping for appliances, look for models with sound control. Many dishwasher models offer quieter operation, and some food waste disposals are wrapped with insulation for less noise vibration. Ask to hear an appliance running before purchasing it.

26

Minimize vibrations.

To prevent your heavy appliances like the washer, dryer, or refrigerator from transferring additional noise vibrations to the supporting floor, place rubber pads under each leg or corner of the appliance. Allow at least two inches between the wall and your appliance, and between your washer and dryer, to eliminate banging noises.

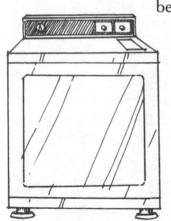

Nurture, don't nag.

Nurturing nourishes, or stimulates growth, in others; nagging annoys, or drives others farther and farther away, if not physically, at least emotionally. If you struggle with nagging, strive to make a request once, then drop it. Turn your frustrations over to the Lord, and try to focus on encouraging the ones you love.

28

Soak up the sound.

*F*or a quieter home, choose furniture, fabrics, and finishes that absorb sound. Upholstered furniture and lined fabric draperies enhance quietness. Carpet is the best sound absorber for floors, but wood floors absorb

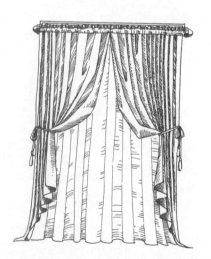

more noise than do vinyl, tile, or stone. Add area rugs to hard surface flooring to soften noise. Quiet walls by paneling or upholstering them.

Make a memory.

*U*se an audio or videotape player to record special moments in your home. Tape your child's comments after her first day of school. Interview a grandparent or parent about their past and your family history. Tape record your husband reading the Christmas story in front of a crackling fire. The familiar sounds of a loved one's voice will keep precious memories alive.

30

Get an earful
of reality.

*I*f you want a real earful of the sounds that fill your home, run a tape recorder unannounced during mealtime or any busy time in your home. Play it back to your family for a good laugh — and maybe to point out areas that could use improvement.

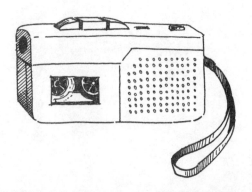

Add an aquarium.

*F*or a lovely, tranquil sound, set up an aquarium in a prominent spot in your home. The colorful fish swimming in their exotic surroundings will captivate your eyes, and the soothing hum of the motor running will calm your soul.

32

Avoid the television trap.

*T*elevision can be one of the greatest detriments to healthy relationships in a home. Turn off the tube and tune into each other's lives to bring calmness and consideration to your home.

Set up a super sound system.

$\mathcal{E}$xcellent sound can greatly enhance the atmosphere of your home, so buy the best sound system you can afford. Wire speakers into several adjoining rooms so you can experience great sound as you enjoy your whole home.

34

Blast off.

*F*or a great sound while viewing a video or television, hook up your television to your stereo speakers. The resulting sound will be fuller, richer, and louder. You'll feel like you're sitting in a theater or stadium!

Know about
newsworthy news.

*K*eep current on world happenings
through one news medium; listen to or read
about news just once a day. It's good to be
informed, but there's no need to inundate
your mind with unimportant, irrelevant, or
destructive information.

36

Be a sport.

Celebrate the seasons by occasionally listening to a sports game being broadcasted. Whether on radio or television, swing into spring by listening to a baseball game or kick off fall by filling your home with the sounds of football. Even if you are not an avid sports fan, show love to those with whom you live by sitting down with them and getting into the sights and sounds of the game.

Round up the ringers.

*B*egin a collection of pretty handbells with pleasing rings. Mix old treasures found at flea markets or antique shops with new ones discovered in gift shops or on family vacations. Display your beautiful bells, filled with memories, in a little spot looking for a charming touch of sound.

38

Be considerate and compromise.

For the most pleasant atmosphere, it is best to have only one sound maker on at a time. Inevitably, however, where two or more are gathered, there will be times when different people have different sound preferences. In such situations, be considerate and compromise. Use a headset. Take turns selecting music. Close doors. Turn the volume down.

Save those special sayings.

When your child is young, keep a special book to record his or her inquisitive questions, hilarious sayings, and profound words. Chances are, you'll remember these sayings for a while as you relay them to others, but as life goes on, they'll be forgotten. Present the book to your child when he or she leaves the nest.

40

Snap, crackle, pop!

*I*f you have a fireplace, take advantage of the cozy sound of a crackling fire by lighting one often. Burn only dry wood that's been cut and seasoned for at least nine months. For an extra pop, occasionally toss in a pine branch or cone.

Make time for "couch time."

Make it a habit to set aside some time most evenings to sit down on the sofa and talk face-to-face with loved ones. Turn off distractions, put away projects and paperwork, and enjoy quality conversation.

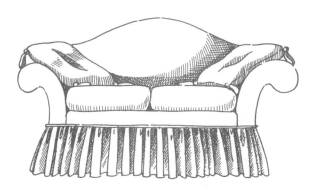

42

Jingle your pillows.

Stitch a bowed bell on each corner of a square pillow. Every time it's tossed, it will jingle. Make holiday jingle pillows and give them as Christmas gifts.

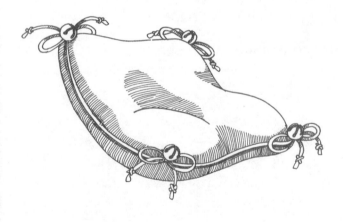

Retreat for rest.

*N*o matter what our age, there are moments when we are tired, irritable, and unpleasant, and whatever comes out of our mouths is likely to be the same. Have a family understanding that when someone is unpleasant, they be excused to the quietness of their bedroom for the rest they need. This will save many hurtful and unnecessary comments.

44

Love by listening.

Show others your love and concern by listening carefully to them and not interrupting their thoughts. Put down what you are doing and give them your undivided attention. You may hear something very important, or at least convey to them that they are important to you.

Say pretty please.

Set a good example for your family by using the word "please" as a part of your everyday vocabulary. "Please" softens a statement by turning it into a respectful request. People are much more likely to respond to a considerate comment than a command.

46

Have a humble heart.

We all blow it now and then, especially with those who we love the most. Keep a clean slate in your home by apologizing sincerely as soon after the incident as possible. Humble words like, "I'm sorry, will you forgive me?" can heal a broken heart and prevent walls of bitterness and resentment from building. Be an example to your children or spouse and humble yourself.

Lighten up and laugh.

$\mathcal{L}$ike a ray of sunshine, laughter lightens life's load by brightening outlooks and broadening perspectives. Lighten up and laugh in your home, especially at yourself. Rent a funny movie, relax, and enjoy your home life with those you love.

48

Skip the sarcasm.

*H*ealthy humor helps, but unhealthy humor hurts. Sarcasm is cut-down humor, or humor at the expense of others; it may start out being funny, but it ends up being destructive. Do a sound check on the sarcasm in your home, starting with your own tongue.

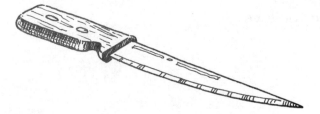

Tune in
to your tone.

*K*eep a close check on the tone of voice in which you communicate in your home. Tone and volume say much more than words and can enrich or ruin a home's atmosphere.

50

Relive memories with music.

*K*eep a variety of different types of music that remind you of magical moments in your life. Buy a CD or cassette of the sound track to a fabulous movie or favorite musician of a concert you attended. During a romantic evening, play a special song that reminds you of your courtship. When reminiscing, play music from the era in which you grew up.

Make Christmas merry with music.

$\mathscr{C}$elebrate the holidays by filling your home with your favorite Christmas songs all season long. Play one as you pull out your decorations. Turn one on when you curl up in front of a late-night fire. Praise God as you listen to songs that cause you to reflect on the miracle of Jesus' birth.

52

Keep it soft and subtle.

*W*hen entertaining, soft music is a wonderful backdrop to relax guests and fill in awkward gaps of silence. Though music can enhance the moment, make sure conversation can be shared without strain.

53

Say hello!

*Y*our phone is your line to the outside world, so answer it with warmth and enthusiasm. Ministering to others means being kind and considerate, no matter how you feel or who is on the other line. If you can't handle it, don't answer it.

54

Communicate with convenience.

A cordless phone or a phone with a long cord will give you flexibility to do easy, quiet tasks, like ironing, while talking. Save time by making all your calls at one time. Simplify your life by never making a trip somewhere when a quick call will do.

Please leave a message . . .

*H*ave an answering machine to take a message when you're away from home or when you simply do not want to be disturbed by the outside world. There are many varieties on the market; choose one that has the features you desire. Make your greeting pleasant and friendly. Keep your answering machine in a convenient spot where it won't disrupt conversation with family or friends.

56

Ring, ring.

*I*f you're in the market for a new telephone, don't skimp on quality. Buy one with clear reception as well as a pleasant ring. Ask to hear a telephone's ring before you purchase it. A sudden, shrieking phone can unravel the nerves, so when you get it home, set the ring volume as low as possible, but still at a level you can hear.

Blow smoke.

$\mathcal{T}$urning on a noisy exhaust fan over the stove can sound like a plane getting ready for take off! Run your fan on the lowest level needed. If you're in the market for an exhaust fan, be aware that most fans have a numeric rating: the lower the rating, the quieter the sound.

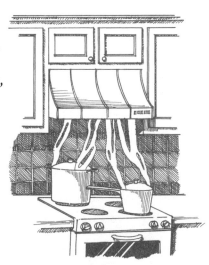

58

Quiet countertop clamor.

$\mathcal{K}$itchen countertop appliances not only add convenience, but they can also add unnerving noise. The better the quality, the quieter an appliance is apt to be. When operating, reduce the sound of churning blenders or beating mixers by wrapping the motorized area with a dish towel or placing the appliance on an absorbant mat.

Turn on the timer.

When cooking, use a timer rather than continuing to open your oven door or pot lid. Set the timer for a minute or two before suggested cooking time; when it goes off, peek once for doneness.

60

Keep your cabinets quiet.

*B*ecause wood and laminate cabinets reflect kitchen sounds, putting dishes away can sound like a bull in a china shop. Soften the sound of clanging dishware by placing rubber or cork tile on the shelves of your kitchen cabinets. To 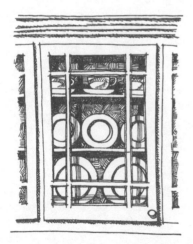 make closing the cabinets quieter, use soft, rubber or cork bumpers on the inside edges of doors and drawers.

Whistle away.

*B*uy a pretty teapot that whistles. When
you need hot water, fill it up and listen —
it will sing to you when your water
is boiling.

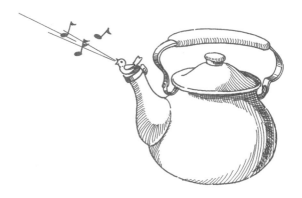

62

Listen while you work.

To make the most of time spent doing chores around the house, listen with your ears while you work with your hands. Upbeat music will motivate you to move quickly while cleaning. Christian teaching will make time spent ironing or cooking seem to go faster.

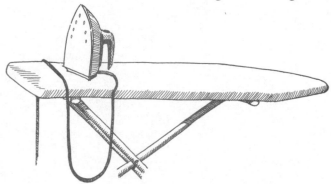

Have book ears.

*I*f you can't seem to find time to read, but want to enjoy a best-selling book, many are available on audiotape. Purchase an audio book at a bookstore, rent one, or check one out of a local library. Enjoy listening as you do tedious tasks around your home.

64

Cherish kitchen chats.

We can nourish others in our kitchen with encouraging conversation just as well as with delicious food. Kitchens are a natural gathering place for homework, paperwork, or just sitting and talking. Make the most of opportunities for casual kitchen chats. While you stir a hot pot of soup, someone may be warming up to open their heart.

Ding for dinner!

*A*void the strain and sound of shouting throughout your home for others to come to dinner. Instead, have a familiar, pleasant-sounding dinner bell that signals dinner is almost ready. By the time loved ones wrap up what they're doing, dinner will be ready, and no one's nerves will be shot.

66

Let it ring.

*T*ry to not answer the telephone during any meal, but especially during dinner. If the eating experience is to be calming and enjoyable, interruptions that can interfere with conversation and digestion should be avoided.

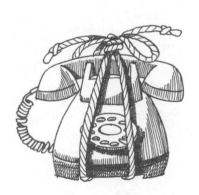

Make the most of mealtimes.

*T*ake every opportunity to sit down with others and eat together. If necessary, give young children a nap and a snack to tide them over so your family can eat at the same time. Try to keep the atmosphere positive: turn off the television, play peaceful music, and save heavy subjects for another time.

Make an effort to include everyone in mealtime conversations.

68

Bring on the bells and whistles!

$\mathcal{K}$eep fun party noisemakers on hand for an instant sound celebration. Pull them out for birthdays, special announcements, and to ring in the New Year!

Serve foods that sound scrumptious.

*T*ry crispy chips, crunchy vegetables, popping corn, or sizzling steaks. Pleasant-sounding foods enhance the satisfaction and memory of a snack or meal.

70

Have an attitude of gratitude.

*B*egin every meal with a brief prayer of thanks to God for his provision of food. Take turns saying the mealtime prayer. No matter how few or simple the words, a prayerful pause will help everyone to reflect on God's goodness.

Thank you! Thank you!

An attitude of gratefulness should carry over into our family relationships. Thank family members for doing the dishes, making their beds, and emptying the trash. Knowing their little efforts are noticed and appreciated will encourage them to keep helping.

72

House a feathered friend.

*E*njoy the sweet chirp of a canary or the smart talk of a parakeet in your home. Keep your bird in a decorative birdcage and let its song and chatter become a part of your home's familiar sounds.

Help the sick and tired.

*A*long with many illnesses come the sounds of coughs, sneezes, sniffles, blows, moans, and groans. Keep plenty of medicine on hand. To help clear your head when congested, steam the air with the soothing sound of a vaporizer. If you are sick and sleep with a mate, show consideration by sleeping in another room. This will keep your spouse healthy and rested.

74

Have a "get-well bell."

Spoil a sick loved one with a designated "get-well bell" beside the bed. Whenever he or she needs something, a simple ring will let you know. This soothing sound and a little "TLC" is sure to help cure any mild illness.

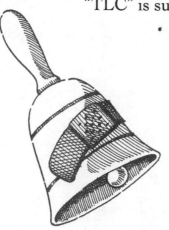

75

Nod off naturally.

*O*n a rainy night, open the windows and let the peaceful sound of the rain pouring soothe you to sleep. In the autumn, drift off to sleep listening to the rustling leaves falling from the trees. Let the sweet sound of birds singing outside your bedroom be your wake-up call.

76

Cut out creaking.

*I*f your mattress creaks or squeaks when you roll over in it, it's time to replace it. Purchase a quality, quiet mattress and box spring set and get a good night's sleep.

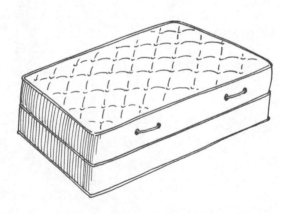

Shed tears and heartaches.

$\mathcal{S}$ome of our most painful, yet precious moments in life are when we have wept in the safety and comfort of our homes. Tears can be healing. Make your home a comforting place where family or friends feel the freedom to shed tears and heartaches.

78

Drift into dreamland.

*H*ave a clock radio with a sleep button. Set your radio on soft, soothing music and drift off to sleep. The sleep button will play twenty minutes or so of your favorite music before it shuts off automatically. If all goes well, you'll never hear it stop.

Tune it out.

*I*f there's no escaping distracting noises while you're trying to sleep, wear a pair of comfortable earplugs or mask the noise with a constant humming sound, such as an air conditioner, small fan, or space heater. Or try a sleep machine that continuously plays recordings of pleasant nature sounds to help you fall into a deep sleep.

80

Do not disturb.

*B*e sensitive and considerate to those sleeping. Tiptoe quietly. Whisper to others when nearby the sleeper. Turn off the telephone ringer in adjacent rooms. If you must wake up in the morning before your mate, lay out your clothes the night before and place them in the bathroom.

Forget the phone after bedtime.

*A*fter you have retired to your bedroom for the night, avoid taking phone calls. Talking on the telephone forces you to reenter the world, prevents you from mentally unwinding for a restful night's sleep, and keeps you from getting to bed on time. If someone calls in the middle of the night, consider it an emergency; if they call late in the evening, consider it impolite.

Wake up on the right side.

*T*he way in which you wake up can set the tone for your whole day. Set your clock radio to wake you in the most pleasing way possible. Listen to a radio station that plays music you enjoy — if you're a light sleeper, keep the volume soft; if you're a heavy sleeper, turn it up loud. Set a CD-playing alarm clock so you can wake up with a grateful heart, listening to praise music.

Snore no more.

*I*f you are a snorer, or sleep with a snorer, chances are you're not getting a restful night's sleep. For a quieter night, get a contoured snore pillow for the snorer. The foam pillow cradles the head and neck to allow proper breathing and peaceful sleeping. (If all else fails, investigate surgery to correct the snoring problem.)

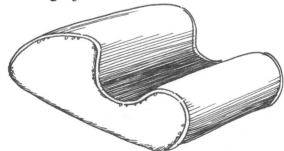

84

Be well-read.

$\mathcal{M}$ake it a family ritual to read aloud to one another. Read a Scripture or devotional thought at the breakfast table, a Bible verse to a loved one once you've crawled into bed, or an interesting article to stimulate discussion. As much as possible, read books to children or let them read them to you.

Good readers make leaders.

Look it up.

*D*on't miss a chance to expand your
vocabulary. Keep a good dictionary and
thesaurus beside your bed. When you are
reading in bed and come across an unfamiliar
word, look it up. Then begin using it in your
vocabulary as often as possible.

86

Plan a peace talk.

Though it's best to settle disagreements before going to bed, there are those weary nights when further discussion only adds to the frustration. If this is the case, set a time and place for a peace talk. Once you are rested, refreshed, and have gained a proper perspective, resume your discussion and deal with the issue. Never avoid resolving an issue. A soothing home is a peaceful home.

Say a prayer.

$\mathcal{M}$ake it a nightly ritual to kneel at your young child's bedside for prayers, and also pray out loud beside or in your own bed before you go to sleep. Even a short prayer of thanks for the day lets God know you haven't forgotten his hand in your life.

Take time for tuck-in talks.

Cherish your children's tender years by treasuring the times that you tuck them into bed. Secure in the comfort and quiet of their beds, they are often willing to open their hearts to you. Listen, laugh, and shower them with love. Every now and then tape record one of your tuck-in talks and save it to listen to after they've become too big to tuck in.

Savor the sound of silence.

Every now and then, turn off every sound maker and enjoy the precious sound of silence. It will clear the air and your mind. You may even hear something you would have missed amidst the noise.

90

Treasure quiet time with God.

Guard your quiet time with God, as it sets the tone for your whole day. Get up early for time alone to read, write in a journal, or pray. The more time you spend with God in quiet solitude, the clearer you will hear his voice leading you through the busyness and noise of your day.

Stop the
drip-drops.

*E*liminate the irritating sound and waste of water by fixing leaky faucets and running toilets. If possible, learn a few plumbing tips and do simple repairs yourself.

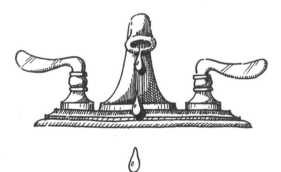

92

Hush the flush.

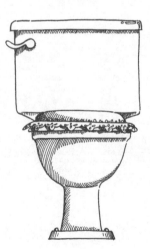

For a quieter-sounding flush, buy or make a lovely fabric padded cover for your toilet seat lid. The fabric will absorb and soften the sound of flushing water. If you are purchasing or replacing a toilet, keep sound in mind as you make your selection.

Fill your days with praise.

$\mathcal{M}$ake your home a place of praise. Listen to praise music as you get dressed in the morning. Play praise tapes or CDs and meditate on their worshipful words during your quiet time. Sing a praise song out loud when you feel it in your heart, or let one minister to your heart when your spirits need a lift.

94

Store it in your heart.

Store up the treasure of God's Word in your heart and mind by memorizing Scripture. Listen to Scripture memory melodies to learn verses. Hang a memory verse on your bathroom mirror and quote it out loud several times while getting ready for the day.

1 COR. 13: 7
love hopeth
all things

Sing in the shower.

When standing under a sprinkling shower, go ahead and belt out a musical melody. Whatever others think doesn't matter. We all think we sound pretty good in the shower. Give your day a lift by lifting your voice.

96

Bring a song along.

*P*ortable tape or CD players travel with ease to your bedroom or bathroom. Select music appropriate to the mood you are trying to set. Listen to romantic, peaceful, easy-listening music as you turn in for the day; upbeat music while getting dressed to go out on the town; fun music during children's bath time. Allow kids to keep a simple tape recorder in their room to listen to tapes while they play or rest.

Make music.

*I*f you or those you love enjoy playing an instrument, determine appropriate times and places for practicing. Whether it's the piano, guitar, flute, or other instrument, making music can make your home beautiful.

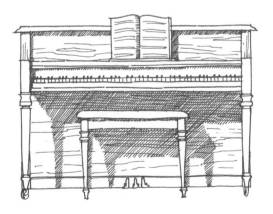

98

Wind up a memory.

*F*or a touch of beauty and music, place a pretty music box in a little spot where it will welcome others to wind it up. Hang a music mobile that plays a favorite lullaby from your baby's crib. The soothing sound will please baby's ears.

Wash away your cares.

Water relaxes us not only with its touch against our skin, but also with its sound to our ears. After a long, difficult day, turn on the bath water and listen to its peaceful sound as it rushes out the faucet. Let the water wash away your cares as it fills the tub.

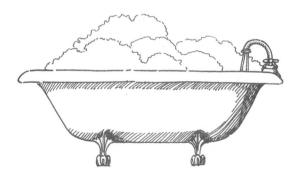

100

Tap, tap.

*F*or a hospitable sound, mount a small door
knocker on your powder room door. When
guests fill your home, the light tap of the
knocker will help determine if anyone is
behind the closed door. Visitors will find the sweet
touch delightful.

101

Tame your tongue.

Though every sound with which we fill our homes affects its atmosphere, none can be more soothing or saddening than our words. Spend time in God's Word studying the many Scriptures that refer to the powerful influence of the tongue. Use a concordance to help you locate appropriate passages. Ask God to help you build your home with loving and encouraging words.